MW01234194

i

This is my second book. I have discovered the unlimited joy of writing and sharing ideas and knowledge. @NCWiseman

Success Using Social Media

Starts With Building Relationships

by Teddy Burriss

ISBN: 9780988915534

DEDICATION

Thanks to my wife, Rebecca, for giving me all the time I needed to make this book become a reality and for pushing me to stay focused on completing it.

I've been encouraged by many of my friends to write this book, about a subject I am passionate about and have been teaching for quite some time.

Thanks to my many friends, both IRL (in real life) & on social media for the encouragement and ideas that helped me to collect the many stories and examples I share here.

CONTENTS

Thank you my friends

I want to thank everyone involved in encouraging me to get involved on social media. I don't recall who the first person was to tell me to join Facebook, LinkedIn, Twitter, Google+, YouTube, Blogging, FourSquare, Tout, Pinterest, Posterous, etc, however, please know, I am grateful for the nudge.

I have met, virtually as well as in real life (IRL), many great social media extraordinaires. They share useful and enjoyable content, engage with us, and most of all, are sociable and caring people.

By early 2013 I had met 1000+ people on Facebook, 1000+ on Twitter, 3000+ people on LinkedIn, (not including all of the great people in Groups I engage in) and countless others through other social media platforms like FourSquare, Tout, Vine, InstaGram, Pinterest and about.me. Yes, some of my friends connect with me through more than one platform, however, the number of people I have met virtually is very high just the same.

I am blessed to have been able to turn many of my social media relationships into fantastic IRL relationships. People like Jon, Ade, Ann, Kim, Kristen, Paul, Lisa, Scott, Laura, Connie, Jessie, Jamie and John, are just a few who come to mind that have become great friends for life.

There are different and unique groups on Facebook, Twitter and Google+ who say good morning to each other each day. These unique, encouraging and inspiring activities often help us to get our day started in a more positive manner. I get to meet new good people through these simple social media interactions.

I am grateful for all of relationships I have built with my fans, followers, friends, connections and subscribers.

I'm also grateful for the technical support and development teams of the various social media platforms I use. They are smart people who care and want to help us be successful with their products.

Connecting with good people, having good conversations that build into fabulous relationships in well designed and managed social media platforms make for good times and great opportunities.

Thank you everyone.

Why did I write this book?

I'm often asked, "Why do you spend so much time on social media?"

There is more than one answer to this question.

I use social media to learn, teach, have conversations with others, share stories and compassion, as well as to entertain and to be entertained. I use social media to discover new ideas and to share my ideas, to stay in touch with other people and to keep others informed of what is going on in my life, where relevant and useful. I used social media to thank others for their help, congratulate others on their successes, accomplishments and other life events.

When I roll this all up into one nice neat statement it is:

"I use social media to build relationships."

~ @ NCWiseman

Compared to many of my friends and business peers, I started late using social media. I did not create my first blog post until November 2004, my Facebook account until August 2007 and my LinkedIn account until August 2008. I am LinkedIn member 29,287,147. I sent my first tweet in late 2008. I did not create my first Facebook Fan Page and Group, LinkedIn company Page and Group until sometime in 2010.

In 2009, while doing the research for my first book, "*Networking for Mutual Benefit*," I realized social media could play a significant role in my life, career, business and community.

At first, I thought blogging was just a way of capturing my stories I wanted my family to know about. I thought Facebook was just a good way to keep track of my daughters who were still in college. Once I joined LinkedIn, I came up with a bigger idea.

As I started building my LinkedIn Profile and connecting with people, I asked myself these questions:

- Why can't I use Facebook and LinkedIn to connect with people for life?

- Why does LinkedIn have to be only for business and Facebook only for family and friends?

- Why can't I use social media to make connections for life, career, business, and community?

It took a while for me to work through the idea, but eventually I came up with this personal philosophy of social media:

> *"I will use any and all social media platforms to connect and build relationships for life, career, family and community."*
>
> ~ @NCWiseman.

If I was serious about building relationships, why not use social media to help me do this. The thought of only building relationships "IRL" − in real life − seemed so limiting. I could build relationships virtually through social media and if possible turn them IRL. This seemed to be a great way to expand my reach and connections to people. It was clear to me that social media would help me to find, develop, and nurture relationships that mutually move people forward through life. Wow, I thought this would be fabulous, and it has been.

While putting together this plan, I thought about the issue some have, "I want my personal life to be separate from my business life." I thought about this for a while and again asked myself some big questions:

- "Why keep my personal life and business life so separated?" I'm one person, one set of knowledge, ideas, experiences, passion and moral compass.

- "Why would I separate my social media content into unconnected buckets?" I thought through the pros and cons and came up with my answer. I decided I will not have unique and separate social media identities.

It became clear to me that merging my social media life into a single entity would create better success for my career, community and business., i.e. my life. It was an easy decision for me.

I shared this idea with some friends (business and personal). Many were not as excited about this idea as I was. I heard concerns like:

- What if you say the wrong thing?

- What happens if someone in business sees a picture you don't want them to see?

- Do you really want your business contacts to see your personal information?

- Do you really want your mother-in-law to see who you do business with?

- I would never let my business connections see who my family is.

- Your business connections are not going to connect with you on Facebook.

- Lots of other negative ideas filled with fear and doubt.

Some of these concerns had merit. I didn't want anyone to see pictures of me that shouldn't be seen by everyone. Another concern was, I didn't want to say the wrong thing and hurt anyone or my reputation.

These concerns got me to thinking about what's important:

- Nothing I do on social media will hurt anyone.

- I will always strive to help or give through social media.

- Everything I do through social media will always be good stuff.

- The core activities that guide my social media work will focus on building relationships.

- I will never let social media replace the opportunity for an IRL experience with anyone.

These statements seemed rather easy for me to do. The more I thought them through, the more sense they made to me. I eventually came up with this edict:

"Never do, say, or engage in social media in a way you don't want to be seen, heard, or perceived in life."

~ @NCWiseman.

Wow - this philosophy should help keep me out of

trouble.

I did not figure out how to do all the right stuff through social media on my own. Really, I was not a professional social media person and even today, I refuse to use the word "Expert." How can you be an expert when everything is constantly changing and new ideas develop every day. I have decided the best way to refer to myself is as a "proven authority." The people I coach and teach social media to trust and respect me because I am honest about my skills in a fast changing environment.

I have (and continue to find) great sources of social media and relationship knowledge, mostly through fantastic people. Some of these folks are nationally or internationally know. Seth Godin, Guy Kawasaki, Keith Ferazzi, and Mark Schaefer are just a few such sources of knowledge that helped me to create my personal social media policies. Even though they are dead Dale Carnegie and Ralph Waldo Emerson's books have also helped me to improve my social media and relationships building practices. I can name dozens of local people who are also great sources of social media and relationship building knowledge which I benefit from. Elizabeth Cottrell, Kristin Daukas, Scott Dickson, Arminda Lindsay, Jon Lowder, John Lusher, Cheryl Schirillo, Ann Tran and Kim Williams are just a small list of these local folks. I appreciate each of you.

As I studied the Dale Carnegie Principles for my first book, "*Networking for Mutual Benefit*," it became clear his first nine principles were not just important for IRL networking, but also critical to social media relationship building.

Before reading any further, there are two points I want to share with you:

First – While I'm confident you'll find the many of the ideas in this book worth applying to your own life, it's important that you know I consider myself very different than most people. Please don't try to be like me. Just because I have decided to use a large number of social media platforms to connect and build relationships for life, career, business, family and community, does not mean you have to or should consider doing the same. You need to decide which social media platforms are best for you and then use them to help you to connect and build relationships for your life, career, business family and community.

What I truly hope, is that once you read this book you will decide to adopt the principles I share to help you create your **Success Using Social Media** in a way that is beneficial to you and your connections.

Second - This book is not a social media primer. I won't get into a lot of details regarding the individual social media platforms or how to use the many features and functions of each platform. Writing that book would be a great waste of time because the many different social media platforms change quickly and often.

After you read this book, if you want training on using the different social media tools, connect with me through social media to learn about the training I do. I can be reached from my blog, www.ncwiseman.com or by sending an email to NCWiseman@TeddyBurriss.com

I wrote this book to help you create *"Success using Social Media"* that can help you in your life, career, business, family and community.

Social Media Success Stories

Throughout this book I will share with you principles, techniques, ideas, best practices and even how to stay out of danger. All of this is important. However, reading stories of how others have found value from their time and investment in using social media is very important.

Sprinkled through out this book are Social Media Success Stories for you to read how other people have benefitted from using social media.

You will know a Social Media Success Story is next when you see:

Pause and take a moment to read a Social Media Success Story

I hope you enjoy reading these individual stories and benefit from each one in some way or another.

After you read this book, if you have a Social Media Success Story, please share it with me via email at NCWiseman@TeddyBurriss.com. I will add it to the growing list that I publish at www.successusingsocialmedia.com. Include a link to your favorite social media profile and I will include this in the online posting.

What is Social Media?

I'm not going to try to list all of the social media sites for you. They change constantly, and new sites are coming online all the time. My primary social media sites are Facebook, Google+, Instagram, LinkedIn, Pinterest, Tumblr, Wordpress and YouTube. These are only a fraction of the social media sites that exist as of 2013.

Even though I may focus the discussion of this book on my top five or six social media sites, I do not want you to get hung up on which site to use. The ideas in this book will help you get value from any social media site.

Social media platforms are designed for people to engage in social conversations.

"Social media refers to the means of interactions among people in which they create, share, and exchange information and ideas in virtual communities and networks" (source: http://en.wikipedia.org/wiki/Social_media).

Social media platforms are for people to engage in social conversations.

Social media venues are for people to share and benefit from the co-creation of content and ideas.

Social media sites are where people connect and build relationships.

Social media sites are for conversations, not selling.

> *"Social media are tools for us to talk with anyone we want, anytime we want, and about anything we want."*
>
> ~ @NCWiseman

I wrote this definition a few years ago, because I kept hearing business owners and executives tell me, "Social media is managed by our marketing department." I quietly weep every time I hear this. When I hear this statement I have to ask:

"Does marketing manage your phone system?"

"Does marketing manage your email system?"

"Does marketing control the use of your fax machines, pens and pencils?"

"Does marketing escort your staff through life, into networking meetings, coffee shops and bars?"

"If not, why does marketing manage your social media activity?"

Don't misunderstand me, marketing has to be involved in developing content as it relates to the brand and marketing message, regardless of whether it is distributed by paper, email, fax, mail, bar stools, or social media. Social media, however, are "social" platforms from which people can communicate: share ideas, knowledge, introductions, etc.. They're not just for marketing or to share the brand message(s).

Just as many business executives think IT owns the applications, many think that marketing owns social media. These business philosophies are changing, slowly, but they are changing.

For the purposes of this book, social media sites are venues for us to communicate with anyone we want, anytime we want and about any subject we desire.

In this book I will share ideas of how to do this properly.

Which Social Media to use

The philosophies of this book are the same regardless of which social media platform we decide to use, even though I'll be using my favorite sites to illustrate these philosophies.

There are far more social media platforms than any of us will need or want to use. This Wikipedia article lists well over 150 currently in use social media platforms - http://en.wikipedia.org/wiki/List_of_social_networking_websites

I am not going to tell you how many or which social media platforms to be on, but remember there are only so many hours in the day, so make good choices relevant to your own life, career, business or industry and your own targeted audience.

We need to understand a principle that I call <u>SMPR</u> - "Social Media Platform Relevance."

Let me explain further.

First let's look at the public definitions of my favorite platforms:

- **Facebook** - Facebook's mission is to give people the power to share and make the world more open and connected. As of 7/2013 there were 1.06 billion monthly active users on Facebook

- **Google+** - Google+ is Google's foray into social media (besides YouTube). As of early 5/2013 there were 359 million active users and the second largest social network.

- **LinkedIn** - LinkedIn is the world's largest professional network with over 238 million members (7/2013) and growing rapidly. LinkedIn connects you to your trusted contacts and helps you exchange knowledge, ideas, and opportunities with a broader network of professionals.

- **Twitter** – Twitter is a real-time information network that connects you to the latest stories, ideas, opinions and news about what you find interesting. Twitter had 200 million regular users in early 2013

- **WordPress Blogs** are ongoing tours, with human guides. Camaraderie and authentic relationship often develop between a blog's creator and its readers. There are 60 million WordPress sites on the web as of 9/2012.

If we believe in the philosophy that social media is where we communicate with anyone we want, anywhere we want, and any time we want, from 50,000 feet, there is little difference between these three social media platforms, except how they function and the content they share.

However, if we dig a little deeper, here are the defining differences (based on my use of these platforms) that help me define SMPR:

- **Twitter** - Short bursts of useful, engaging, and interesting information relevant to all areas of life.

- **Facebook** and_**Google+** - Posts of fun, heartwarming, compassionate and informative content intended to share, engage and entertain in all areas of career, business and community (life). Our Facebook and Google+ Profiles are extensions of us as a person, while our Facebook and Google+ Pages are extensions of our groups or business.

- **LinkedIn** - Professionally focused content intended to engage, inform and enthuse other professionals in all areas of business. Our LinkedIn Profile is a portal into the professional person we are, while our groups or business Pages are more focused on specific topics and or areas of life, business, career or community.

- **Blogs** - Our stories, ideas and information intended to inform, education and/or entertain the reader.

Why is this differentiation important? Because **SMPR** (Social Media Platform Relevance) guides us not to share all the personal stuff on LinkedIn and not to share all of the "heavy" business stuff on our personal Facebook timeline. SMPR is also important on your Google+ Profiles and Pages, as well as on your blogs. Applying SMPR to everything we post and share will help us be more engaging. Good engagement creates opportunities for real relationships. I'll share more about this since it's at the heart of what is TRUHE.

Keeping SMPR principles in mind, don't hesitate to get onto any or all of the social media platforms that interest you. Just be careful of the time constraints. A body has to eat, sleep and watch football, so use social media efficiently and productively.

Why build Relationships through Social Media?

When I first started teaching this subject, I was often asked, "Why should I use social media to build relationships?" Some really old school sales people actually said, "I don't have time to build relationships, I'm trying to make a living."

Usually this question about social media comes from people who knew how to build lifelong "in real life" (IRL) relationships. You know who these folks are; they are at every networking event and they regularly email and/or call the people in their contact list. These people have powerful relationships with the people in their circles.

My answer back then is the same as my answer is today,

> *"Social media expands our reach into new industries, communities, regions and worlds. It creates opportunities to meet new people we can help and who can help us."*
>
> ~ @NCWiseman.

I agree that an IRL relationship trumps a social media relationship every time, but IRL relationships are restricted by time, distance and budget. Social media relationships are only restricted by Internet connectivity, which is growing faster than roads and airplane routes.

Because of my face-to-face networking, seminars and public speaking, the number of new relationships in my IRL network is increasing, on average, by 5-10 new people every day. Because of the rapid growth and adoption of social media, the number of new connections in my social media networks is increasing by thousands of new potential relationships every day.

Another statement I hear is, "There is no way I can connect with enough real people on social media to help my business." I agree, if we use social media the same way many collect business cards, there is no value to getting involved on social media.

> *"If we use social media as a new business card collection system, we will fail miserably in business, career and community."*
>
> ~ @NCWiseMan

I figured out how to use social media to create relationships that have turned into much more than just a connection. It takes time, a little energy, being a little vulnerable, and being willing to focus on the other person. It works, it has turbo-charged my business, and I want to teach you how to do this too.

My involvement on social media has allowed me to help others find solutions to problems, connect with other people where relevant and useful, find jobs, work, and start new businesses.

I have made new business connections, found resources to help me with my online programs and books, developed new ideas, and been hired to do consulting work and public speaking engagements. All because of my social media connections, relationships and relevant activity.

Another benefit of building relationships on social

media is that often I get to turn a virtual connection into an IRL connection. Since an IRL relationship can be a stronger relationship than a virtual one, this is important to me. It happens often, and enriches my life when it does.

None of this could happen through social media if I did not first build some level of trust and respect with my connections. I prove daily that building relationships through social media is a fabulous benefit to my career, business and community, i.e., my life.

To summarize this chapter, building relationships through social media can help us to create success.

SUCCESS /sək'ses/ - noun

1. The accomplishment of an aim or purpose

"Strive not to be a success, but rather to be of value." ~ Albert Einstein

"Action is the foundational key to success." ~ Pablo Picasso

> *"Success occurs when you give to others first, focus on your goal and never stop striving to achieve."*
>
> *~ @NCWiseman*

Pause and take a moment to read a Social Media Success Story

Elizabeth H. Cottrell Success Story

@Riverwoodwriter

RiverwoodWriter.com

linkedin.com/in/elizabethcottrell

How appropriate to be sharing a social media success story with Teddy Burriss, because social media is responsible for our knowing each other and discovering that we are kindred spirits! My sister in Winston-Salem told me about a young blogger there named Cyndi Briggs whom I started to follow and admire. Before too long, Cyndi introduced me, by social media, to her friend Teddy Burriss. Since Teddy walks his talk, he immediately set up a phone call, which consisted primarily of him finding out about me and my work so he could try to help me through his own connections. I was impressed.

Finding Community

But I also want to share with you the role that social media has had in connecting me with a whole community of like-minded, heart-centered business men and women who are passionate about their work, generous with their time and talent, and making a difference in the world. It all started with my own interest in online business and participating in a few courses and webinars. I soon identified online experts and mentors whom I respected and followed from afar. Last fall, I participated in one of Laura West's "30-Day Passion Projects." Much to my delight, several of the women whom I've long admired as successful internet entrepreneurs were fellow classmates, and we interacted regularly in the class's Facebook group over the course of the 30 days! Through this experience, I got on their radar screen and they have taught and encouraged me immeasurably ever since.

Powerful connection tools

I've come to believe this about social media tools and platforms:

They are a powerful means of connection when used appropriately and authentically.

They often provide an opportunity to interact with leaders and celebrities in your field who would otherwise be inaccessible.

In a very real sense, they bring us full circle back to two or three generations ago when a handshake was all it took to seal a deal and our reputation was everything. The principles are the same, but social media provides the means to greatly broaden our reach and amplify our message.

Teddy and I have never met in person, but thanks to the power of social media, we are already discussing how we can collaborate to help as many people as possible achieve their dreams. It just doesn't get any better than that.

by Teddy Burriss

What is TRUHE?

TRUHE /trōo/ - Verb

1. To use social media in a way that cultivates mutually beneficial relationships that create value and opportunities.

"Three things cannot be long hidden: the sun, the moon and the truth." ~ *Budda*

"Anyone who doesn't take truth seriously in small matters, cannot be trusted in large ones either." ~ *Albert Einstein*

"If you tell the truth, you don't have to remember anything." ~ *Mark Twain*

> *"TRUHE, Transparent, Relevant, Useful, Honest and Engaging, is a fundamental guideline for life and social media."*
>
> ~ @NCWiseman

I will always be indebted to Thelma Elaine Carter for her help creating TRUHE. More on this later.

Not only are the individual words of TRUHE important, but the word itself, TRUHE, although spelled uniquely, is equally as important. We live life hoping everything we see, hear and participate in is TRUHE. We need to participate in being TRUHE as well.

Some people don't care about the truth and use

technology to manipulate us. This causes us to worry that what we see, hear and engage in online (and in life) may not be TRUHE. Once we discover that someone is not being TRUHE, we discount their value and eventually ignore them altogether. When our connections begin to ignore us, it becomes very difficult to build their trust again. Being ignored can occur in life as well as on social media, therefore we need to be TRUHE in real life as well as on social media.

However, if we are always TRUHE in life and on social media, our connections will learn they can trust and respect us. They then begin to pay attention to what we have to create, what we share, and what we think. This trust and respect is critical for us to be able to build powerful and mutually beneficial relationships with the people we connect with on social media.

Read the next five chapters and learn how to be TRUHE in all aspects of your life.

Always be Transparent

trans·par·ent /trans'pe(ə)rənt/ - Adjective

1. Easy to perceive or detect

2. Nothing to hide

"I felt that it's best just to be as transparent as possible." ~ *Rupert Murdoch*

"A lack of transparency results in distrust and a deep sense of insecurity." ~ *Dalai Lama*

"I wonder what his real agenda is?"

We often ask this, or think it, because we have been conditioned not to trust people we don't know. To make matters worse, we have experienced people who were hiding something, using smoke and mirror tactics in business, or pretending to care about us when they really didn't.

This whole distrust we have for the people we don't know (and the reciprocal distrust others have for us until they get to know us), makes it difficult to build relationships through social media. That's why it's so important to make sure our social media activity is completely transparent.

Transparency can be produced in a number of ways:

- **Profile Picture** - If you tweet, you know about the egg, a twitter profile without a profile picture. Unless we know who the person is, we generally do not trust Twitter profiles with an egg. This is true with LinkedIn, Facebook and Google+ as well. If we are willing to show a photo of ourselves on social media, we are making ourselves just a little more vulnerable, thus transparent and more trustworthy.

• **Profile Descriptions** - We refer to these as our BIOs. A well-written BIO helps to create transparency. Personal BIOs that describe us as an individual, instead of the company we work for, are more transparent. We can learn about the businesses through the experience section of your profile, LinkedIn company pages, Facebook pages, or company websites. Our Profiles need to be all about us as individuals, professionally and personally.

• **Status Posts** - Posting Status updates, Discussions, Tweets, Videos, etc, are important ways to give to others. However, if our posts are regularly ads or promotional material, this is not a gift. Furthermore, if we post something that pretends to be a gift, and in reality it's only a sham to get our connections to pay attention to our promotional material or sign up for our lists. These activities are not going to help us build relationships on social media either. It's ok to post a self-promotion or advertisement periodically, but it needs to be clearly declared as an ad.

• **Connection Requests** - Following people on Twitter and YouTube is rather easy. In general, there is no need to ask permission. Even on Facebook and Google+, we can subscribe to a member's public content. On Facebook, LinkedIn and Google+, in order to effectively engage with our connections we have to send a friend or connection request. It may sound counter intuitive, but you should only send connection requests to people who know us and we know them. Furthermore, only send these requests with the focus on making the connection, nothing more. Requesting a connection of someone with the intent of going to the "sales" step next will not work. social media is not where we sell.

Being transparent in life and with our social media activity is important when we are trying to build mutually beneficial relationships.

Always be Relevant

rel ·e ·vant /'reləvənt/ - Adjective

1. Closely connected or appropriate to the matter at hand

2. Pertinent to the subject

"What's most galvanizing for me is the opportunity to be topical and relevant and entertaining. That's the holy grail." ~ *Kathryn Bigelow*

My wife reminds me often about the importance of relevance, "Teddy, we are not talking about motorcycles right now, we're talking about your daughter's baby shower." I usually shut up and listen at this point.

Relevance on social media applies to specific discussions, posts, hashtags, groups, communities and pages.

Here are a few tips that help us to stay relevant:

- **Page and Group Profiles** - When we create a Facebook Page or Group, LinkedIn Group, Google + Circle, Pinterest Board, blog, etc, we should use the features of the platform to publish our purpose. When we inform our audience of the purpose through the name, title, description, about section, and rules, they are more likely to stay relevant to the subject of our page, group, etc when they engage with us and the other members or our groups and pages.

- **Blog Comments** - Commenting on a blog article we read is a great way to build a relationship with the author, host, and even others who read the articles. If the article is about gardening, we should not comment and redirect people to our totally irrelevant blog about monster trucks. Not only will we be ignored, we will be considered rude.

- **Stick to the discussion** - When engaging in a discussion on social media, stick to the original topic. It's rude to change the conversation in mid thread. Besides being rude, if the conversation is about football and we throw in a statement about tires, we're likely to be ignored. We should not throw in a question to one of the participants of the conversation either. It's not appropriate to join a conversation and ask, "How are you doing Steve?" If we have something else to talk about, or a question to ask someone directly, we need to do this in another conversation or a private message.

- **Stick to the topic** - Additionally, when having a conversation in a Group, Community, Page or Hangout remember that these areas of social media are also generally focused to a specific topic. Sharing a story about a paralegal issue on a project management business page would not be relevant. Likewise, we should not start a conversation about property management in a warehouse distribution Google+ Community. Keeping our conversations relevant is important if we want to build relationships on social media.

- **Tag properly** - We should not tag people on social media for the sake of sharing our message far and wide. We should only tag people relevant to the conversation, image, video or link. Additionally, because our connections can tag us on just about any thing, we should always pay attention to what content we are being tagged in.

- **Event Invitations** - Facebook has a good event-sharing feature. It works well with Eventbrite.com and Doodle.com. I use it regularly, as do many of my connections. One disappointment is when thousands of people are invited to a Facebook event that is either in a different city or state, or worse yet, for a program or event that is totally irrelevant to those invited. I don't have enough fingers and toes to count the number of invites I've gotten to jewelry parties, tupperware parties, political action meetings, bar mitzvahs in other countries and even bridal showers in different states. We need to be deliberate and relevant when inviting our connections to our events.

When we stay relevant on social media, our connections are more likely to pay attention to what we share. This is important when we are trying to build relationships through social media.

Pause and take a moment to read a Social Media Success Story

by Teddy Burriss

Ira Bass Success Story

@IBMedia

ibmedia.biz

linkedin.com/in/ibmedia

As the saying goes, "things happen for a reason." One of those "things" happened to me on 4/19/07 and as it turned out, it did happen for a reason. I was fired. After just 8 months on the job and having been fully relocated, I was asked to leave. Immediately.

I thought to myself, "No problem. I'll take a breather and just slide right into my next adventure." But, there was a problem at the time. It was called the pre-Recession.

Over the next several months I started to consult until I could find my next position. The license plate on my car, IB MEDIA became my calling card and company name. With 30 years of advertising media experience I had the experience ad agencies wanted as they were letting their employees go. I could be a hired gun advertising professional.

Here's the rub. I never wanted this. An entrepreneur? Networking? Cold calls? Always looking for work? I'm a pretty outgoing guy, but the thought of standing around with a drink in my hand or cold calling to peddle my skills did not excite me.

Then it happened! I discovered this new social media platform. Not Facebook. Not Twitter. LinkedIn! Back in 2008 there were ~30,000,000 registered users. A far cry from today's (7/13) 225,000,000 members. However,

37

I saw huge potential in it's efficacy.

I was excited! I taught myself the ins and outs of LinkedIn and I began to connect with marketing professionals in my immediate vicinity, Charlotte, North Carolina. The coffee meetings started to flow. I began to meet new people and as I did I kept thinking that there are former colleagues and clients who I also needed to reconnect with. The people from my past who had no idea what I was doing now. And so I did.

Paul Mason was a former client of mine. I thoroughly enjoyed working with him. When our companies and the agency I was working for at the time parted ways, we lost touch. Fear not! I searched for Paul on LinkedIn and there he was. We reconnected. We spoke and emailed each other on occasion until one day he gave me some great news. He had just taken a position at Johnson Controls in Milwaukee, Wisconsin.

In one of the messages from Paul, he said, "Ira, the company is reviewing their media planning and buying needs. I'd like to introduce you to the decision makers." My heart pounded with excitement. LinkedIn was working for me.

Long story, shortened, I earned the assignment! At the time, the acquisition of this large company's media planning changed my life. Its impact on the success of my company continues to be felt daily.

This is my story of how social media has had an absolute vast impact on the success of IB Media LLC (www.IBMedia.biz). The way I see it, reconnecting and building relationships on social media helped me go from vapor to gaining multi-million dollar clients.

Always be Useful

use ·ful /'yŏŏsfəl/ - Adjective

1. Able to be used for a practical purpose or in several ways.

"Do not be too moral. You may cheat yourself out of much life so, aim above morality. Be not simply good, be good for something." ~ Henry David Thoreau

My wife helps me pay attention to what is useful. When we were raising our four daughters, I often put my foot in my mouth or said something totally useless. By the time they were grown, I had learned everything I needed to know to properly raise daughters. I'm sure I was a good dad, but with age and training, now I am much more useful.

Usefulness is important when using social media as well. There are many different ways to be useful. We can be useful with what we share, how we engage in discussions and how we connect.

Here are a few ways we should strive to be useful on social media:

- **Sharing knowledge** - Share articles we find on other websites that may be useful to our connections, whether on Facebook, Twitter, Google + or LinkedIn. If the articles contain useful information for a group, share these articles directly into the group instead of on our main wall or timeline. Sharing on social media has gotten very simple and is a great way to provide useful information for our connections to benefit from.

- **Use Third Party Content** - We are not the only source of useful information - Just because we love to write and share our own stories, articles and knowledge, does not mean we are the only source of good useful content. Rather, strive to share useful information from others more often than we share our own content. This helps to show we are not selfish and all about ourselves and we pay attention to other sources of great content. Besides, despite what we want to believe, our content is not always the best. (I deny writing that out loud.)

- **Sharing and responding** - When one of our connections starts a discussion or asks a question, strive to share it with others and respond appropriately. When done appropriately, this is useful to both our connection and those we share the discussion or question with. Only do this when it's beneficial and relevant to all involved.

- **Helping people to connect** - Be very deliberate about connecting people on social media. This activity is useful when we know someone has a need and another connection may be able to fill the need, or help find a solution. Connecting people where relevant and mutually beneficial is a powerful way to "give" and giving is a great way to be useful on social media. Be honest about this connecting activity. If we connect two people where there is no relevance or honesty, we could jeopardize our relationships.

- **Motivation and inspiration** - We can get lots of value reading other motivational and inspirational material. Sharing this content through social media can be equally as useful to others. Appropriately shared motivational and inspirational content can be very uplifting to our connections on social media. Unless you are the Dali Lama or Dale Carnegie, however, don't start spouting motivational and inspirational posts all day long. Too much of a good thing in the wrong place could turn people off and cause them to ignore you. Additionally, social media is not your pulpit and no one wants to read your sermons all day long.

These are only a few of the ways we could be seen as useful on social media. Being useful will add great value to our connections and help to build real relationships.

Always be Honest

hon ·est /'änistē/ - Adjective

1. To do or be with integrity, sincerity, candour

2. To be trustworthy

"Be yourself; everyone else is already taken." ~ *Oscar Wilde*

"If you do not tell the truth about yourself you cannot tell it about other people." ~ *Virginia Woolf*

"Truth never damages a cause that is just." ~ *Mahatma Gandhi*

> *"Honesty is an important trait in life. It's also a requirement when using social media."*
>
> ~ @NCWiseman

As we work to make connections and build relationships through social media, honesty will be assumed and expected. Our connections will be disappointed if we do something less than honest on social media. Once our connections discover our dishonesty, it will become a major task to repair the damage we have caused.

I hope we don't need to have a conversation regarding how to be honest. We know how to be honest, and we should practice it with no hesitation.

Here are some less than honest social media activities we should never do:

- Share an article we know is not true, hoping it will make us or our business look better

- Share content we have not read or viewed completely ourself. We need to know exactly what we are sharing with our connections

- Gossip about anyone or any business. This will not help us or our business

- Tell rude jokes or share distasteful content. Most of our connections will think badly of this activity. It's not worth the risk of offending the majority of our connections for the sake of a few who will laugh at an inappropriate joke

Again I reference Dale Carnegie's principle #12, "If we are wrong, admit it quickly and emphatically." If we either by accident or intentionally share content that is less than honest, we should publicly correct ourselves and apologize. Then, never share dishonest content again.

Honesty is required in every relationship, including the relationships we are trying to build on social media.

Pause and take a moment to read a Social Media Success Story

By Teddy Burriss

Amy Howell Success Story

@howellmarketing

howell-marketing.com

linkedin.com/in/amyhowell

Engaging with Influence: How I met some of my most valued advisors, mentors & key business contacts through Twitter

For me, Twitter is an awesome way to find and connect with key business contacts. I often tell my clients that it is more about finding the right kinds of people than it is broadcasting content. Content is important but it is the people you can meet that matters the most. One shining example is meeting Anne D. Gallaher who owns a PR firm in Harrisburg, PA. I found Anne on Twitter, started following and talking with her. Fast forward 2 years and we have just collaborated to write and publish our new book, "Women In High Gear." Now this doesn't happen overnight but over time and some quality time spent together. Once you connect through the social channels, it's important to connect in real life. Anne and I have become good friends and now business partners in our writing and speaking. Our book is the product of our relationship and a continual value to our businesses.

Another important connection is my friend Mark W. Schaefer, also someone I found on Twitter. When traveling to Knoxville in 2009, I called Mark and told him I was coming to his town and wanted to meet him. Since then, we have met in real life many times and have created a "virtual crew" of talent we can tap if needed. Really powerful and today's way of cutting through clutter to get to what you are looking for. For me, Twitter

45

has been a way for me to find people who add value to what I am doing for my clients.

When social media was new to most people (back in 2009) there weren't many courses or experts to turn to in my home town of Memphis, TN. I knew running my PR firm that if I wanted to stay relevant and keep clients, I had to get in front of the social media sea change. In order to do that, I turned to Twitter to find people who could help me learn, grasp the important things and help me understand how social related to business. Twitter--I think--has become the trip wire for news. If something happens, you can see it on Twitter first. If you are in PR, that is hugely important.

Another example of an important connection through Twitter is my alliance with my legal and social media advisor, Glen D. Gilmore. Glen lives in New Jersey, is a lawyer and social media advocate and I also met him on Twitter. I started following him and decided to call him after concluding he would be someone with whom I'd want to have on my team. After a phone call and some in person meetings, we landed a project working together on social media compliance for an airline client of mine in Memphis. The project lasted for 2 years and since then, I have involved Glen in a number of other projects when appropriate. Like Anne and Mark, Glen has become one of my most valued resources. There is probably not one problem we couldn't figure out how to solve working together.

Meeting these people through Twitter has literally changed the course of my business and life. Geography limits us sometimes to the number of people we can meet. Social media helps break down this barrier and open a whole new world of contacts. What an incredible time we live in!

Always be Engaging

en·gag·ing /en'gājiNG/ - Adjective

1. To be involved, exchanging of ideas and information in a positive and enjoyable manner

"Art is more engaging that propaganda." ~ *Larry Norman*

"Not engaging in ignorance is wisdom." ~ *Bodhidharma*

"I think that you can disagree with people and debate over their positions with issues without engaging in the politics of personal destruction." ~ *Hillary Clinton*

> *"Engaging and exciting is a powerful way to educate and build relationships."*
>
> ~ @NCWiseman

Engaging people in a professional and polite manner is a fabulous way to build relationships IRL as well as through social media. When conversations are interesting and relevant, people want to be a part of them. Engaging with people in relevant conversations helps them feel like a member of a community– valued and useful to others. All of this value is important when you want to build relationships.

Here are a few ways to be engaging on social media:

- **Say Hello** - One of the simplest ways to engage with people on social media is to say hello. We can periodically send relevant messages to the people we see being active on any social media platform. Comment on their activity, congratulate them for a positive career change, thank them for sharing an interesting article or ask them a relevant question. Never ask for anything for yourself. I always offer, "If I can help you in any way, please let me know."

- **Get involved in a discussion** - When someone starts a discussion on social media, either through a Facebook status, a LinkedIn discussion, a Tweet, a Youtube video, blog post or Google+ post, etc, they want us to see it, share it and engage in the conversation with them. We should get involved in their conversations when relevant and useful. Not only will this help build our relationship with them, but we may learn something from them. Stay relevant to the original post and watch how some discussions can just take off and virally invite new people into the conversation.

- **Don't try to over-engage** - LinkedIn allows us to join 50 Groups. We can join Facebook Groups, Google+ Hangouts, Circles, YouTube Channels, etc. Don't over do it. We should be focused and deliberate on where we decide to get involved and engaged. If we try to engage everywhere, we'll diminish our value to others as well as ourselves. If we join a group and decide we are not getting value or providing enough value to others, we need to get out of the group.

- **Invite our connections to participate** - If we join a group on LinkedIn or Facebook, find a good blog to follow or discover a new person on Twitter or Google+, we should try to invite relevant connections to join us. Inviting our connections to these groups or to follow these other social media contributors tells our connections we care about them. We can also politely and relevantly tag our connections in a discussion to encourage them to get involved as well. Again, we should not over do this engagement activity.

• **Don't be all business** - Social media is a place for us to have conversations with our connections about any subject. If we only do business on social media, our connections will miss out on the total package we have to offer. They may also be less interested in who we are and what we want to share. Mix it up some. There is no magical ratio of business and non-business content. This mixture will vary per person and their connections. In real life we use all types of discussions to build relationships. Humor and entertainment play a big role in relationship building, even with our business contacts.

• **Accept differences** - Being engaging on social media requires we accept different points of view or someone possibly saying we are wrong. Politely accept criticism when it occurs. We don't have to accept the point of view or change ours because of what is said, unless we want to. We do need to let people share their opinions, when done politely. We want this respect for our opinions as well, right?

Engaging our connections in discussion, inviting them to participate with us, and sharing some good humor with them will help us to build relationships through social media.

The 5Cs of Social Media

The 5Cs of social media are:

"Contribute, Collaborate, Connect, Cram, and **Create"**

The 5Cs of social media are intended to encourage us to engage, make new connections and learn from our time on social media. Doing this can help us to be trusted, respected and considered an authority in our industry.

I compare the 5Cs of social media to high-octane gasoline. We could use regular gasoline in our cars, but when we use high-octane gasoline, the performance improves significantly. Likewise, we could just have good LinkedIn, Facebook or Google+ profiles. When we use the 5Cs of social media, we'll get much more value out of our social media involvement. The cost is a little higher, yet so are the benefits.

Building relationships through social media really begins to grow once you adopt the principles of the 5Cs of social media.

Let's discuss them a little further.

Contribute on Social Media

con·trib·ute - /kən'tribyoōt/ - Verb

1. Give in order to help others

"It is not what we get. But who we become, what we contribute, that gives meaning to our lives." - *Tony Robbins*

"A man may be a tough, concentrated, successful money-maker and never contribute to his country anything more than a horrible example." - *Robert Menzies*

"Giving is a powerful way to create relationships."

~ @NCWiseman

Building great social media profiles with beautiful profile pictures and blazingly fantastic bios is only the first step towards getting value out of our social media activity. Contributing is the first big value activity needed in order to begin building relationships that help us in life, career, business and community.

Contributing on social media is a form of giving, and when we give to others with no expectations of anything in return, we create an environment for relationships to develop. As I am sure you expect by now, providing TRUHE (Transparent, Relevant, Useful, Honest and Engaging) content is an essential part of giving to our online community.

There are two primary sources of content we can contribute through social media.

Source #1 - Content we create. Self-created content is a great way to show our skills, passion, talents, expertise and experiences. In the past, this often took the form of white papers or case studies. While social media can still be used to share these, most people are interested in content that is more "social" and easier to digest. Here are a few examples of self-created content we may want to share through social media:

- Blog posts containing stories of accomplishment and success in the areas we are an authority in

- Blog posts containing how-to articles, instructions and positive ideas in the area we are an authority in

- LinkedIn or Facebook status updates about interesting ideas or unique questions relevant to our community, area of business, or career

- An interesting, fun and/or useful picture that is relevant to us as a person and/or professional. Maybe a picture of an event or presentation activity. We should use good captions and polite tagging of others when sharing images or articles of others on social media

- A YouTube video that shows a solution to a problem or an interesting concept that video can present well

- An event that would be useful or relevant to others and where we demonstrate our skills and talents

- An entertaining post, story, picture or video that helps others connect with us as a person, not just as a business contact

Source #2 - Third Party Content we have read. Sharing third party content is a great way to contribute. It shows we are not selfish or just "tooting" our own horn. Third party content helps to amplify our value, skills, expertise and experiences, especially when this content is relevant to who we are and what we do. In order to find and share third party content, we need to regularly read online content. Here are some suggestions of third party content to read on a regular basis and share through social media:

- Industry specific sites
- Association sites
- Competitor (or peer) sites
- Local, regional and national news sites
- Community sites
- Government agency sites
- Industry expert personal sites
- YouTube channels

Use email subscriptions or a newsreader to stay informed of updates to the online sources of good content you find useful and interesting. I use a different email address for my online subscriptions. This way I keep the growing list of subscription messages out of my general business or personal email. I also use NewsFire for Mac as my newsreader. I paid for it because I like the features of NewsFire, but there are free newsreaders too.

An important cautionary note, we should never share third party content until we have read it completely. We need to know and understand the content and what it references before we share it. I have read articles that started out with good content, but in the middle of the article, the discussion or point of view changed to something I could not support. Don't get caught sharing something you have not read completely.

Regardless of the source of the content, we need to be deliberate about where we contribute it.

Here are a few examples of where we can contribute good content:

- LinkedIn Profile
- LinkedIn Company Page
- LinkedIn Group(s)
- Twitter feed
- Facebook Timeline
- Facebook Page and Groups
- Google+ Profile and Company Page
- Google+ Hangout(s)
- Pinterest Board
- Blogs (company and personal)
- Other social media platforms appropriate to you and your life, career, business and community

I have only scratched the surface of the types of content we could share and the places where we could share it. Use the Bonus Principle of Experience and Experiment to find more content and ways to contribute. (Oops, I'm a head of myself again. More on this later)

And, just because you can drop the same content onto all of your social media platforms at once does not mean you should. Choose the relevant sites, pages, groups or profiles. And, always remember to be **TRUHE**.

Contributing **TRUHE** content is a great way to build relationships through social media.

Pause and take a moment to read a Social Media Success Story

Mark Tosczak Success Stories

@marktzk

marktzk.com

linkedin.com/in/marktosczak

From Foursquare to Real Life

There's a popular lunch spot near my office, a Mediterranean-style cafe called Zaytoon. I had been using Foursquare more and more, and had gotten into the habit of checking in wherever I went, even if it was only when I walked the 50 feet from my office to the cafe.

One day, I checked in at Zaytoon and got the Foursquare notification indicating that I had "stolen" the mayorship from someone else. The previous mayor's name didn't immediately ring a bell with me, and I didn't give it much thought. I had won mayorships at sorts of places.

But soon after (it must have been that afternoon or the same week), I got a Twitter message from the previous mayor: "Well played, Sir!" it said, congratulating me on winning the mayorship. The person sending the message was David Horne, Zaytoon's previous Foursquare mayor and, I realized, someone I'd met before at Greensboro's ConvergeSouth. A quick check of his online profile and I realized that he, like me, was in the marketing business. David was someone I should probably know better than I did.

So I replied and asked if he'd like to get together for lunch (at Zaytoon, of course). He did, and we did, and we soon became friends. Since then, David and I have volunteered together, worked together and used each other as professional sounding boards to get feedback on ideas and talk about our personal and professional aspirations. It's a relationship that I value, and it was Foursquare that helped make it happen.

Look me up on LinkedIn

In 2007, I was walking down the street a few months after having left The Triad Business Journal and started working at RLF Communications. As a result of leaving the paper, my byline had disappeared from its regular place in the weekly paper, and I had lost touch with some connections I had made at the paper.

A man in a pickup truck at a red light, rolled down his window, and yelled, "Hey Mark." "I haven't seen your name in the paper lately. What have you been up to?"

It was Jonathan Smith, a financial advisor and one of the very first sources I'd interviewed for one of my very first stories when I joined the Business Journal Staff in 2004. I yelled back something about having a new job and saying we should reconnect. But I was acutely aware that at any moment the traffic light was going to turn green and Jonathan was going to drive off. We didn't have time to exchange cards or do anything else. "Google me" I told Jonathan.

He did, and my LinkedIn profile came up right at the top of the search results. That led Jonathan to discovering LinkedIn and signing up for an account. And, of course, we reconnected over a meal later – much more leisurely than yelling at each other in traffic. Jonathan is now my financial advisor.

Contribute Bonus Tip

Nearly all of the websites we visit have social media tools built in that allow us to share what we read with our connections on our social media sites.

Fortunately, these tools usually work the same way on all sites because they are created by the social media platforms. Facebook, LinkedIn, Twitter, Google+, Pinterest are great examples of platforms with really good "sharer" tools. This is important because when we read an article or watch a great video, we should consider sharing it with our connections.

Share only the best articles and videos you find online. We don't call our friends after every article we read on the paper or after every news story we see on television. Likewise, don't share everything you read online with your connections. Be selective and focus on giving great content that can help your connections. I encourage you to experience and experiment with these sharing tools and share really good content with your connections.

Because these website social media sharer tools are so easy to use, building relationships with our connections becomes easier as we share, give, and contribute through social media.

**Pause and take a moment to read a Social
Media Success Story**

by Teddy Burriss

Angel Guerrero Success Story

@aswebpros

aswebpros.com

linkedin.com/in/angelguerrero

By no means is this story the only success I have found using social media, but it is the most amazing reunion story to ever happen to me.

First of all little background. My family immigrated from Guayaquil Ecuador, SA. to New York City, where I was born shortly afterwards. Regularly my Mom, so proud of her son (me!), would mail pictures and heirlooms (a first tooth or two) to her family in Guayaquil Ecuador, SA.

Once a month Mom would call back home, international long distance on a landline. She would spend upwards of 30 minutes each call talking with her family and excited to hear their voices. Imagine, the large Latino family (10-15 people) huddled around the telephone all waiting their turn to talk with their family member in New York City. All under one room, scrambling for the phone to say hello or to hear the echoes of laughter and tears of joy. Each call was a fantastic event.

I made my first visit to the homeland when I was about 8 years old. I was literally treated like a prince. Though my family was very poor, they were very rich in love, hospitality. The stories they told (and could tell) would easily fill a couple of large novels. We stayed for a month, playing on the beaches and shopping centers with my cousin and uncles. I learned what it truly meant to have very little compared to what we had in the NYC projects back home. I learned that the invisible thread of family really never gets cut, regardless of the distance or countries we lived in. I left that country with a lot of memories and promises that one day we would reunite.

Fast forward two decades. Like many others I'm using Facebook as well as other social media tools. I'm connecting with friends, family and business contacts. Being an active Facebook user, I was sharing stories, pictures and updates of my bride and three children.

One day I get a Facebook friend request from Ecuador, Arcardio. I was totally flabbergasted. It was my Uncle. I had no idea they had computers, let alone internet connection in their little poor part of town. We connected and the next day a new journey of reuniting began. During our first Facebook chat my uncle asked if I had a camera on my computer. The next conversation was using video. 20 years after seeing him in real life, I got to see my uncle's face via Skype. It was a very emotional time for both of us. We spoke for over 20 minutes. I introduced him to my bride and children. I saw and spoke with my aunts and other uncles, cousins and their new children. My, what a day! The generations and the ties that bind us are now closer and stronger than ever, despite the distance.

Through the power of social media, after a few months of Skype conversations and Facebook chats we were able to catch up on most of what had happened over the past 20 years with our families.

We now talk, share and chat nearly daily. We share tons of pictures, videos and posts about our families activities and lives. I have been to birthday parties being held in Ecuador, Arcardio through the screen and camera of a laptop sitting on a chair. I get to see, hear, laugh and cry with everyone else nearly as if I were there.

This is a truly amazing story. The generations are now together and we will live our lives together, despite the distance.

I am still planning a return visit. Being a part of their lives through Social media is making the trip all the more meaningful.

Being able to reunite through social media with my family has literally changed my life.

Collaborate on Social Media

col·lab·o·rate /kəˈlabəˌrāt/ - Verb

1. Work jointly on an activity, especially to produce or create something.

"Unity is strength... when there is teamwork and collaboration, wonderful things can be achieved." - Mattie Stepanek

"I think a good relationship is about collaboration." - Jennifer Aniston

"I think it is in collaboration that the nature of art is revealed." - Steve Lacy

When we collaborate on social media, it means to "get involved in the discussion or conversation."

Collaborating starts with paying attention to what our connections share on social media. When we find an interesting or relevant post we should consider reading it, in the hopes of learning something new or interesting. Where appropriate and useful to our connections, as well as ourselves, we should engage in the conversation. This is the essence of collaborating on social media.

When we collaborate online, we are telling our connections we appreciate what they are sharing. We also create the opportunity for a broader discussion about the topic, which often invites others who may bring different perspectives and ideas into the conversation.

In his YouTube video and book "Where Good Ideas Come From," Steve Johnson says;

"We have so many new ways to connect, new ways to reach out and find people who have that missing piece that will complete the idea we are working on, or to stumble serendipitously across some amazing new piece of information that we can use to build and improve our own ideas. That's the real lesson of where good ideas come from, that chance favors the connected mind."

This can occur when we collaborate on social media.

Collaborating on social media is not hard to do and does not need to consume a lot of time. When done correctly, collaborating creates more and more value. Here are a few ideas of how to collaborate on social media:

- Comment on a blog post
- Respond to a question
- Comment on a status, discussion, or article
- Retweet or respond to an interesting and/or relevant tweet
- Comment and/or Like a YouTube Video
- Engage in a discussion in a LinkedIn Group or Company page, Facebook Page or Group, Google+ Page or Community
- Comment or leave your own tip on a Foursquare venue
- Comment and/or +1 a Google+ post

- Repin a Picture on Pinterest
- Share a Facebook event on your own timeline or into a relevant Facebook Page.

As social media platforms change and evolve, so will the nature of your collaboration, but the principles remain the same.

Social media collaboration must be short and simple. If we try to make it more than this, people will get turned off and start to ignore us. Think water cooler conversations, hallway chats, picnic discussions, lunch table or coffee shop conversations. Collaborating in these conversations is not long-winded or complex. Social media conversations shouldn't be either. Remember the word - **"Social**."

An important aspect of collaboration is to stay TRUHE to the thread.

> *"When the social media conversation is about dinosaurs and meteorites, stick to dinosaurs and meteorites. Try to change the direction of the thread and we will exile you from our conversation."*
>
> ~ @NCWiseman

Just like any good conversation can, collaborating on social media helps to build relationships.

Collaborate Bonus Tip #1

Collaboration, when done well, does not include your advertisements or self-promotion.

You may get permission to talk about yourself and your products while collaborating on social media, but you have to wait until you get permission. When you engage properly and regularly, focusing on helping others, eventually you will be trusted and respected by the people with whom you are collaborating. Once the relationship builds to this level of trust, you will get the permission needed to ask, "May I tell you about my company?" The natural progression of these conversations is to take it off of social media and make it IRL.

Collaborating in a manner that helps others, with no expectations of anything in return, will help to build strong social media relationships that allow us to discuss ourselves and our business and create opportunities, at the right time.

**Pause and take a moment to read a Social
Media Success Story**

Jonathan Smith Success Story

@jonathansmith

jonathansmith.com

linkedin.com/in/jonathansmith

To a 6th grade boy in the 1960's in Tennessee, adventure could come and go in the blink of an eye. This story is about how my experience with social media a few years ago sprang from my boyhood adventures.

I lived in a safe, small town. Dad taught Forestry at Sewanee. The 10,000 acre domain, to him, was a science lab, but to me, it was a playground without borders. The technology available to Forestry in those days consisted of weather instruments, surveying gear and reeled tape measures that estimated the number of board feet in a tree. The Monroe calculators were my perennial favorite; at least until the day Dad's department inherited three obsolete hand-crank telephones.

My interest in long distance (then measured by how long it took to ride my bike to the movie theater) took a quantum leap the day those phones appeared at his office doorstep. Ever the teacher, Dad made a make-believe call to show me how they worked.

Obsolete also meant they were doomed to the scrap pile. I begged Dad to let me have these relics and he did. The next day, out of boredom or scientific endeavor (probably not) I cranked one phone's handle as fast as I could. I opened the door. I saw for the first time a generator; a geared armature set inside five horseshoe magnets. The armature spun 100 times faster than my cranking handle. Curiosity blossomed. I touched my fingers to two wires coming off the generator. In an instant, I discovered what 100 volts feels like, entering my body beneath my finger nails; massive lightning bolts. I lugged the wooden phone box up and into my tree-house for more testing. Intrigued with the possibility of communicating with the outside world (consisting of three other sixth grade guys with bikes and firecrackers), I needed to wire my newly found tree-house crank telephone to the outside world. I fetched Dad's extra-long extension cord, snipped off the ends, whittled away insulation and twisted connections until I heard a dial tone. Absent a "rotary dialer" my work-around was to jiggle the switch-hook until an operator took the bait and said, "May I help you?" And I'd respond, "Uh, yes, ma'am, my dialer is broken could you please dial LY8-0232 for me?" To which she reply, "Sure sonny. Be sure to report that broken dialer so we can fix it for you."

Fifty years after that first tree-house crank telephone, my desire to connect with others, in purposes that matter, that give meaning to my life and family, still burns. My tree house based hand crank telephone is long gone. Today's communication tools include social media sites such as LinkedIn, Twitter, and Facebook.

The Lighted Christmas Balls, started seventeen years ago by my then college sophomore daughter Alison, has grown by leaps and bounds in the Triad and beyond, and these new ways of communicating have made their reality richer. Social media communications helped to propel the Lighted Christmas Balls community-wide into hunger awareness and the giving and sharing of countless cans, bags and boxes of non-perishable food for the hungry. The old tree-house crank telephone took on the forms of social media to create, develop and foster many new and fantastic relationships in my life.

Collaborate Bonus Tip #2

"Collaboration does not necessarily mean agreement."

~ @NCWiseman

Because all of us have our own opinions and ideas, we don't always agree. We can also get misled with some social media content, which can be incorrect or down right wrong (i.e. - lies). This creates the opportunity for us to disagree with what we sometimes see on social media.

When we disagree with an article we read on LinkedIn or Google+, a post on Facebook, a blog post, a Tweet, etc., it's acceptable to state our disagreement with the connection who posted it. In fact, I would go so far as to suggest we are somewhat obligated to point out big mistakes. Social media is self-moderated. This means there is no social media police monitoring content we see and share. We must do what we can to help ensure the social media content we share is correct.

Follow these guidelines for expressing disagreement on the content you engage with on social media platforms:

- Share your disagreement directly with the connection who posted the content.

- Politely state you disagree with the statement, article, quote, fact, etc.

- Clearly state why you disagree with it.

- Where possible support your perspective or opinion with additional content from other sources.

- Always   be polite, even when your connection is obviously misled, misleading or just plain foolish.

When we disagree politely, with supporting content, we show our connections we are polite and informed. This helps to show our authority and professionalism in the areas of collaboration.

Pause and take a moment to read a Social Media Success Story

Jeff SanGeorge Success Story

@jeffSanGeorge

jeffsangeorge.com

linkedin.com/in/jeffsangeorge

It was 2005 when I first became intrigued with the world of websites, google and blogs. I also googled myself for the first time.

Every time I did, I found two other people with my name, Jeff SanGeorge. One was Jeff SanGeorge the pro Dirt bike rider, the other, Jeff SanGeorge the Children's book author.

There were other results, but these two were the most interesting and identifiable. However, each time I googled my name I realized that the Jeff SanGeorge that was the most important, me, was missing from the search results. Maybe it was vanity, or maybe it was a sense of the world to come, but I knew I wanted to be in the results for that search. I wasn't sure how to get there, but I knew I would't be professionally riding a dirt bike, or writing a children's book anytime soon!

As the years went by I got very busy in my career and life. I also began to actively blog, network, tweet and use LinkedIn. Slowly my content from blogs, Twitter and LinkedIn began to creep up the pages of my google search results.

In 2009 I received an email that got my attention quickly. It was a standard "Jeff, I'd like to add you to my professional network on LinkedIn" message. The subject of the message was "Jeff SanGeorge wants to connect with you on LinkedIn." Surely this was a bug in

LinkedIn. But it was no mistake, Jeff SanGeorge the Motocross pro and the Children's Book Author (turns out it was the same guy), said he found my profile online and wanted to connect. Wow, this seemed strange, yet so cool.

I accepted the LinkedIn connection request and Jeff sent me another LinkedIn message. He had seen my design work on my online portfolio, and wanted to talk with me about a website design! Wow, Jeff SanGeorge wanted Jeff SanGeorge to do some work for him.

Within a few days I was having a surreal conversation on the phone with the "other" Jeff SanGeorge. We actually had a lot in common, and to make this story even more interestingly, we both grew up in Western New York, within 45 minutes of each other.

Jeff hired me to design a website for one of his clients. The look I got from the bank teller was priceless as I handed her a check to deposit into my bank account.

A few more years went by before Jeff SanGeorge hired me again to do another project for him.

Not only did I find a possible distant relative, because of social media, but I also found a very interesting client.

Now Jeff and I happily share the first page of Google results in a search for "Jeff SanGeorge".

by Teddy Burriss

Connect on Social Media

con ·nect /kə'nekt/ - Verb

1. Bring together or into contact so a real or virtual link is established

2. Join together so as to provide access and communication

"Connecting people to jobs and to each other is absolutely vital to a city's economy (and to the wider economy)." - Lucy Powell

"What tribes are, is a very simple concept that goes back 50 million years. It's about leading and connecting people and ideas. And it's something that people have wanted forever." - Seth Godin

"A connection does not make a relationship. Relationships occur when you engage with your connections."

~ @NCWiseman

"Social media is a great place to connect with people of all types, don't limit our connections to only people who can buy our widgets or are just like us."

~ @NCWiseman

Growing your circles of connections is beneficial in many ways.

Here are few:

- Discover individuals with similar and new interests
- Discover new ideas that can help us in life, career, business and community
- Create bridges through our connections to people and businesses we want or should meet
- Get happier. There are studies that have proven the more friends we have, the happier we will be. For me, this alone sounds like a great reason to grow our circle of connections

In order to grow our circles of connections, we need to regularly make new connections. Social media is just one place where we need to do this. Expand this connection activity into IRL and the benefits are factorially greater.

Important Tip - Please don't think becoming a massive connector on social media will propel your career or life. We have to connect IRL as well as on social media.

Here are a few of the current ways we can connect on social media:

- **Facebook** - Request and accept Friend Requests and Like Pages (we can often subscribe to public people as well)
- **LinkedIn** - Request and accept LinkedIn Connections and Follow Company Pages
- **Google+** - Add people and Pages to our Circles

- **YouTube** - Subscribe to YouTube Channels
- **Twitter** - Follow Twitter members
- **Pinterest** - Follow Pinterest Members and/or specific Boards

Each social media platform has its unique way of connecting. What's important is to connect, when we can, and with people who are interesting, knowledgeable and relevant to who we are and what we do in life, career, business, and community.

Deliberate, focused connections, made with authenticity and a spirit of service, can turn into opportunities to become friends, associates, employers, clients, etc.

Often I hear these statements:

"My business is a niche market."

"There are not many people using social media who need my services or products."

"I can't find anyone to connect to."

I think this is sad.

If the only people we try to connect with in life and on social media are people we hope to do business with, life will be very boring. Furthermore, we have no idea how well connected people are and who they could connect us to. We have to think beyond just business.

Frequently I get help from my social media connections who are stay-at-home mothers, preschool teachers, retired administrators, or ministers. I am as thankful for being connected to these folks as I am for my professional connections.

There are four activities that are important with regards to connecting on social media:

Activity # 1 - Make and accept connections. Don't just accept new connection requests that show up. Send out relevant and useful connection requests yourself.

My personal policy for connecting on social media is that I:

- Send Facebook Friend requests only to people with whom I've had an enjoyable face-face conversation.

- Accept Facebook Friend requests from people I know and have met virtually or in real life.

- Send LinkedIn connection requests to people I know. Knowing people is a broad term (more on this later).

- Accept LinkedIn connection requests only after I determine their relevance to me as an individual. Relevance is a broad term (more on this later).

- Follow people on Twitter once I find them to be interesting and trustworthy

- Put people in my Google+ Circles once I find them to be interesting and trustworthy

- Follow interesting, relevant, and useful business pages (LinkedIn, Google+, Facebook).

(I reserve the right to alter my own policy when I see the benefit.)

Activity #2 - Introduce our connections to each

other when mutually beneficial.

A benefit we can provide to our connections is letting them know if another of our connections might be helpful to them. Sharing this information lets us provide introductions where relevant and mutually beneficial.

Making social media introductions is a powerful way to build relationships. We should strive to do this whenever possible.

When we make win-win introductions between our connections, they will remember what we did for them. Sometimes they will even reciprocate, but that is not the reason to do it. This connection activity helps us to build relationships with the people we connect.

Activity #3 - Respect and care for our connections.

Periodically a new connection will ask me, "How about look at your connections and pick four or five you think need my services. Give me their contact information so I can contact them." I don't like this type of connecting and will not participate in it. I call this "harvesting connections," and we should refuse to treat our connections this way.

I hear about people who join groups or connect with another person with the primary intent of getting to a sales conversation with someone else. I have seen people join groups, send a LinkedIn connection request, and then leave the group. Harvesting connections in this manner will not help us to build relationships through social media. Focus on making connections that develop into even the simplest of relationships before you "ask" for anything. You'll be far more successful.

Activity #4 - Engage our connections

Collecting business cards and social media connections will not help our career or business, unless we engage with our connections.

We should pay attention to what our connections are doing and, when we can, comment on their posts, share their information, or just simply "Like" it to show them we read it.

When we find useful information we think our connections will benefit from, share it with them, either publicly or privately.

When our connections ask for help on social media, we should strive to do whatever we can to help. An introduction to a resource or another connection is a great way to help our connections.

And most importantly, when we can, try to meet our connections IRL. Turning our social media connections into real life connections amplifies the relationships.

Connecting is a big step in building relationships on social media that can help us in life, career, business, and community. Connecting and engaging will lead to reaping the benefits as the relationships grow.

Connecting Bonus Tip #1

#1 - Knowing people is a broad term, with different nuances online than IRL. We should be deliberate about only connecting with people we know. However we also want to connect with people we don't know yet, whom we can help, or who can help us.

On LinkedIn, we can use our existing connections to help us to meet the people we don't already know. Here is an example of an email we could send asking to get connected to an executive of a large organization:

> *"Hello Steve. I hope you are doing well and business is good. I am trying to connect with Bill CEO. I see you are a direct connection to him.*
> *Do you know Bill well enough to advise me as to whether he might be a good connection for me? If not, that's fine, but if you do, and you feel it's appropriate, would you consider helping me connect with him? One way might be to send Bill an email and copy me on it. In the email, you could introduce me to Bill regarding the social media work I do with businesses in his industry and ask him if he would accept a connection request from me.*
> *I appreciate any help you might give me with this connection activity.*
> *Let me know if I can help you in any way.*
>
> *Teddy"*

Getting introduced by a good connection to another good person is a much better way to connect to people we don't know. It starts the relationship building process and is far more personal than LinkedIn Introductions and Inmails. For me, this is a better way to get to know people I don't know yet.

#2 - Relevance is a broad term. We want to connect with people who are relevant to us in any way possible. This includes business, community, career, industry, family, friends, hobbies, etc. It's our responsibility to tell the people we want to connect with what the relevance is.

Often I get social media connection requests without any relevance at all. They give me no clue why they want to connect or why I might be interested in connecting with them. I used to spend time looking for or asking for the relevance. However, our world is too fast-paced and busy to do this all the time, so I rarely spend this energy any longer.

I share this with you, because if we want to make a connection with someone on social media, we need to give them some relevance for the connection request. Tell them where you met, if you have, and why you want to connect. Make sure your purpose for connecting is focused on making a connection for mutually beneficial reasons and not because "I have the biggest new business deal ever." We're more likely to make the connection if we make it honest and relevant. (Oh yeah - TRUHE).

If you've sent a connection request to someone who did not respond, try again, and this time make the request relevant and mutually beneficial.

#3 - How to ask for a connection - At the risk of being repetitious, let me emphasize that it's important to know the person you are trying to connect with and to offer relevance in the connection request.

Another important point about requesting a connection, regardless of which social media platform, is to never ask for anything beyond making the connection.

I've seen Facebook messages, LinkedIn connect requests and emails asking for YouTube subscribers, Twitter followers and Page likes that start off with, "I have the answer to all of your personal and business problems. Follow me on xyz social media platform."

I delete these requests and messages without acting on them. Why? Because we need to make a connection that can turn into even the simplest of relationships before we talk business or sales. Stand true to the fact your connections are important and not "targets" on social media.

It all starts with a relevant connection request. After being seen as TRUHE, it could turn into a relationship. Only then do we get permission to ask for something.

Connecting on social media creates the opportunity to build relationships that can become mutually beneficial. Make the connection first.

Pause and take a moment to read a Social Media Success Story

Kim Williams Success Story

@williamskim

kimewilliams.com

linkedin.com/in/kimevanswilliams

While writing this book a good friend, Mr. Kim E. Williams sent this to me. It's not a social media success story per se, however, I am sure that everyone getting success from their use of social media will agree with it:

"Social Media IS selling but it is the branding, marketing and positioning part of selling. You don't present or close sales on social media." - Kim E. Williams

I recently conducted a Sales Training seminar for a national account on Networking for Sales People in the Digital Age. The greatest "AHA" was that the new breed of decision maker is as likely to welcome communication through text message or social media as email or voicemail. If you want to communicate to this generation of leaders, go where they are listening. Moreover, know that they ARE researching you and your company via social media and Personal Online Profiles before deciding to talk with you.

Connecting Bonus Tip #2

One of the greatest benefits of connecting on social media is the diversity of connections we can make.

Diversity of our connections:

- is what helps us to find new solutions , a new job, new business possibilities, and new friends.

- can help us find new products, resources, business tools and even employees.

- can be a source of new conversations, music, books or movie ideas, vacation possibilities and even ideas for a different car, pet, hair style or home decorations.

- can be fuel for a better life, career, business or community.

There is tremendous value in having diversity in our connections, both IRL as well as on social media. It's essential not to allow limit to this diversity. When we limit our connections to specific groups of people, we create a barrier to the possibilities that diversity can create.

In early 2013 I talked with a young professional who said, "I will not connect with anyone on LinkedIn who is not a customer or potential customer. I don't want to connect with people who can not become a client of mine." I quietly wept when I heard this.

We have no idea how the people in our lives can help us in our career, business or community. Limiting our connections limits the possibilities.

Just on LinkedIn, I am connected to professionals in Information Technology, Marketing, Non-Profits, Human Resources, Training, Public Speaking, Healthcare, Management Consulting, Computer Software, Staffing and Federal, State, County, City Public Offices and more. The diversity of these industries has been immensely useful to me over the past five years.

Regularly I get an introduction to a new connection in a different industry, state or city by an existing connection that I had no idea could make this particular connection for me. This is the power of the diversity of our connections IRL, as well as on social media.

Welcome and cherish the diversity of your connections.

Cram on Social Media

cram /kram/ - Verb

1. The act of attempting to learn large amounts of information in a short period of time.

2. Learning from content provided by others.

3. Cramming is the educational slang for research.

"If you steal from one it's considered plagiarism; if you steal from many it's research" - *Wilson Mizner*

"Research is formalized curiosity. It is poking and prying with a purpose." - *Zora Neale Hurston*

"Cramming is a vital social media activity used to improve our professional and personal selves. When we ignore the knowledge available to us on social media, we diminish social media's value."

~ @NCWiseman

Social media is not only a great place to contribute, collaborate and connect. It is also an important research tool. Research is important in life, career, business and community.

Here are a few areas of social media in which we can do research:

- The articles shared through LinkedIn, Facebook, Twitter, Google+, etc are a fantastic source of knowledge, insights, solutions and ideas.

- Google+ Communities and LinkedIn Groups are good sources of knowledge specific to a topic or issue. Some of the members of these communities/groups are industry experts and worthy of following and paying close attention to their contributions.

- Twitter is a great place to search for #hashtags related to specific topics and learn from the people who tweet the relevant information.

- Facebook Pages and Google+ Pages are worth tapping into for specific content that can help with topics as wide-ranging as cooking, camping, technological ideas, political and religious information and product information.

- We can use LinkedIn and Facebook to pay attention to what specific companies and brands are doing (including our competitors).

- LinkedIn company pages are a great source of information regarding individuals changing positions or companies.

- LinkedIn newsfeed is great for seeing who has joined LinkedIn, joined specific groups, been recommended or endorsed, and made new connections in LinkedIn. These new people could be great resources for us and our other connections.

- Most of the social media platforms are a never-ending source of marketing, sales, and social media articles, infographics, statistics, and videos that can help us with our life, career, business, and community

- YouTube videos have become more informative and entertaining than most other social media sites, providing answers to lots of life, career and business questions on just about any topic. Some of the channels on YouTube are so useful and entertaining you will want to subscribe to them

I read all the time. I read online articles, e-books and stories my social media connections share with me. It is such an immense source of content, I have to bookmark useful articles for reading later. I can't over emphasize the value of this content.

My regular listing of blogs has grown to over fifty individual sites. I have set up a blog reader (NewsFire) to manage this list and have organized them into categories so I can get through them in a timely manner. Some would say, reduce the list. I say, manage a great list of blog sites and learn every day.

I love the knowledge, insights, ideas and philosophies I get from my social media cramming. It has helped me personally and professionally, and it has helped me help others. We can learn and develop personally and professionally as we Cram in the immense amount of content available to us on social media.

Social Media Cramming Rocks!

Pause and take a moment to read a Social Media Success Story

by Teddy Burriss

Jana Carroll Success Story

linkedin.com/in/janacarroll

I had an old photo of three little boys and two slightly older young girls that I took way back when I was a volunteer in the Peace Corps. Hoping someone would recognize these children, I posted it on a Facebook page for the village in Saudi Arabia. Two of the little boys, all grown up, living and working in another country, tagged themselves in the picture.

I had no idea where they were or what they were doing. Now I do. I am so glad to be able to know this after so many years.

I'm glad to see that social media could bring us back together after such a long time.

Create on Social Media

cre·ate /krē'āt/ - Verb

1. Cause (something) to happen as a result of one's actions

2. Bring (something) into existence: "I created a relationship"

"Write it. Shoot it. Publish it. Crochet it, sauté it, whatever. MAKE." -Joss Whedon

"In creating, the only hard thing is to begin; a grass-blade's no easier to make than an oak. " - James Russel Lowell

> *"When you contribute, collaborate, connect, cram and create on social media, you produce value and opportunities."*
>
> ~ @NCWiseman

You create success only when you create consistently. This is true with building relationships on social media.

I coached a business owner on building a LinkedIn profile and engaging with his connections and groups. It was a nine-hour seminar across three days. He wrote a great review about the class and thanked me repeatedly for teaching him how to use LinkedIn. This was a big investment for him. I saw him about three months later and asked him how it was going. He told me he had given up on LinkedIn. He said he could not see any value in using it.

WHAT?

I was not sure how this could have happened. I asked him to tell me more. We sat down and looked at his profile. He had a nice looking profile, but fewer than a hundred connections and very little activity in the past three months. I asked him what he had been doing and his response was, "Not much." I agreed LinkedIn was a worthless business tool if he did not use it. I had to coach him on consistency. It took a few more months, but eventually he changed his opinion. With a higher level of activity he eventually found value from his use of LinkedIn.

To get value out of any business tool, we have to use it regularly and correctly. We can't just get it and set it up. We have to find a way to use the tool on a regular basis. We have to create continually.

Developing a process of creating continually on social media is the only way the opportunity for success can occur. One way to create continually is to schedule time every day to do this work. Put it on your calendar and stick to it. Personally, I live by my calendar. If it's on there, I do it.

One example of doing this comes from a good friend of mine, Adrienne Cregar Jandler of Atlantic Webworks. She has a plan she calls "LinkedIn in 15 minutes a day." I frequently share Adrienne's plan and encourage everyone to use it as a template for the specific activities they want to do on social media, not just LinkedIn.

LinkedIn in 15 minutes a day (Adrienne Cregar Jandler)

(I inserted the LinkedIn tasks that I do daily)

- Monday– (15 Min)
  - Task # 1 - Accept new LinkedIn connection requests
  - Task # 2 - Respond back with standard thank you reply
  - Task # 3 - Review all new notifications
  - Task # 4 - Say hello to 4-5 connections
- Tuesday– (15 Min)
  - Task # 1 - Review Group activities
  - Task # 2 - Read 2-3 articles in LinkedIn News
  - Task # 3 - Share a good article from my best news source
  - Task # 4 - Comment on 2-3 connections discussions
- Wednesday– (15 Min)
  - Task # 1 - Read 3-4 Articles shared by connections
  - Task # 2 - Ask a relevant question in 1-2 Groups
  - Task # 3 - Invite 1-2 connections to coffee, sweet tea or soda
  - Task # 4 - Address any new LinkedIn messages
- Thursday– (15 Min)
  - Task # 1 - Send LinkedIn connection requests to new IRL contacts
  - Task # 2 - Review all new notifications
  - Task # 3 - Start a new discussion relevant to my business

- Task # 4 - Research new companies and people in my industry
- Friday– (15 Min)
  - Task # 1 - Review connection changes
  - Task # 2 - Review who has looked at my Profile
  - Task # 3 - Address any new LinkedIn messages
  - Task # 4 - Review my LinkedIn Profile for any changes or enhancements.

Modify these activities to meet your individual needs. Also pay attention to changes to the social media platforms you are using. It is very likely that these activities could need changing based on the changes to the platforms.

Mix up the activities so each day you are doing something different with your Groups, Pages, Profile, etc. If you dedicate this time each week, to contributing, collaborating, connecting and cramming, you will get value out of your social media investment.

Of course, if you are going to use multiple social media platforms you may need to increase the amount of time and/or add additional daily activities. If you create a calendar of activities and you see some value, then maybe you'll consider increasing your investment. If you don't see any value, then evaluate what you are doing and make changes. Don't give up.

The bottom line is that in order to get value out of any business activity, we have to schedule and commit.

I learned from my Dale Carnegie coach that Practice makes Permanence. Creating continuously will create permanence and improved positive results from your social media involvement.

Social Media Principles

There are many stories, parables, old wives' tales, and powerful words that I use to guide my life. Often these have become principles I strive to live by.

Many of these principles not only keep me between the lines in life, they also help me with my social media activity. They are important individually, but even more powerful as a group of guiding principles. As I began to adopt these principles into my social media activity, I starting getting more value out of my efforts.

Someone once asked me, "Do you judge others who don't follow your social media principles?"

No, I don't, but if you've been in one of my classes, presentations, seminars or read my books, I hope you will adopt at least some of these principles. My goal as a teacher is to create social media users who are different, more authentic, and more effective than everyone else.

These 10 principles are a big part of implementing this goal.

Note - I would love to know if you have any different principles that have helped you create Success using Social Media. Please share via email at NCWiseman@Teddyburriss.com.

Pause and take a moment to read a Social Media Success Story

Mitch Miles Success Story

@mitchmiles

gothe262.com

linkedin.com/in/mitchmiles

Thank You Facebook: Reconnect and Keynote Speaker

On May 11th 2011, I received a Facebook invitation from my preschool and elementary school friend, Carla Harrison (now Turner). Carla and I were born only days apart from one another in Wilmington, North Carolina; we attended preschool, elementary and middle schools together. We had not spoken or even corresponded through email in over twenty two years, and because of the social media platform Facebook, we were able to connect, catch up on careers, share photos, and even see each other's family in a matter of minutes. The ease and convenience of Facebook allowed this reconnection to happen.

One year later, I received a Facebook message from Carla. She was part of the 2012 North Carolina Association of Public Health Nursing Administrators (NCAPHNA) Annual Conference planning committee. One of her roles was to find conference speakers. Having followed my Facebook posts, comments, and updates regarding the social media classes I teach at local community colleges, she wanted to find out my availability of leading a breakout session on the opening day of the conference. She was comfortable from what she read online that I would be able to focus the session on an overview of social media for nurse administrators.

I was thrilled to hear from her and even more thrilled she was asking me to share one of my passions; how individuals and organizations can connect with their patients/clients and employees using social medias like Facebook. I confirmed my availability with her.

Fast forward to the afternoon before the conference. I received several urgent voicemails from Carla and the president of the conference asking me to call them as soon as possible. It turned out the keynote speaker was nowhere to be found and they wanted me to be ready, "if needed," to take the role as keynote speaker. A Facebook connection created the opportunity for a 45-minute breakout session that was leading into a 2-hour keynote presentation.

As I had hoped, they called me the morning of conference opening and told me I was now the Keynote presenter. I had great time and I got to reconnect in-person with my lifelong friend. She happily introduced me to the attendees as the Keynote speaker.

Share your purpose, your passion, and heart on Social media – you never know who and when you may see the fruit of sharing – as for me, in this case, it took 42 years.

#1: The Core Principle of all Networking

"Networking is finding, developing, and nurturing relationships that mutually move people forward through life."

~ @NCWiseman

If we apply this edict in real life as well as on social media, we will build great relationships that over time will become mutually beneficial. I have no expectations from the relationships I build on social media, but I know they are worthwhile to me. Often the benefit of these relationships is not apparent until months or years later.

Finding people on social media is rather easy. All of the social media platforms have features built into them to do this. The real work happens once they become a fan/follower/friend/connection. Developing and nurturing the relationship with them takes time, but it happens when our focus is on them, not ourselves.

We can develop and nurture our social media connections by always sharing good content and regularly offering to help them. When we do this work, eventually we will see our relationships grow. When relationships grow, the mutual benefits begin to happen.

Don't try to turn every connection into a deep relationship; this won't happen. If we follow the principles in this book, the connections with the most potential to develop into real relationships will do so.

#2: Success starts by being Mutually Beneficial

"Networking for Mutual Benefit is a requirement for success."

~ @NCWiseman

I originally created this principle for IRL networking. As I got more involved in social media, I quickly realized it is equally important here as well.

We set ourselves up to fail if we engage on social media to sell our stuff, promote ourselves, or lobby for our mission, without considering this principle.

If everything we do on social media is mutually beneficial to others, we'll find our fans, followers, circles and connections will be more interested in what we post/share and more likely to engage with us. This, then, helps to grow relationships.

Some of my professional social media peers use an 80/20 rule. 80% of what we share must be information, ideas, discussions that are not about us or our business. The remaining 20% can include self or business promoting posts. I strive to push past the 80% guideline. For me, the more I give, the more I get back.

I also try to never talk about myself when I am making connections on social media. I strive to connect with others in a helpful manner first. As I develop the relationship, then I consider sharing a little more about myself and my business.

As I shared in my first book Networking for Mutual Benefit, I never ask for anything until after I get permission to ask. In both real life and on social media, this permission only occurs after the relationship develops.

Mutually beneficial connections are an important principle for networking through social media. Done properly, success occurs.

Not every connection you make on social media will accept the "mutually beneficial" concept. Don't let this stop you from staying true to this principle.

Reminder - "Networking for Mutual Benefit" is my first book. It is the core of all of the social media activities that I teach.

The concept of practicing *Networking for Mutual Benefit* in your social media activities creates the greatest value in social networking.

**Pause and take a moment to read a Social
Media Success Story**

Ray Mitchell Success Story

@raymundmitchell

sixfourweb.com

linkedin.com/in/raymundmitchell

So, Teddy called to ask me a favor. He's says, "You know, I'm working on this book and I'm looking for people who have started good relationships through social media, or have gotten business using social media. Do you know anybody?" I had to laugh, because although it's been some time, the only reason Teddy had my phone number is because of social media.

Years ago, I had started using Twitter to promote a business venture and to engage with other people while developing my online persona. I met Teddy at a Tweet-up after exchanging tweets for some time. People around town had always said "Do you know Teddy Burriss? Have you met Teddy Burriss?" Well I hadn't, so when the opportunity came up and a great friendship began.

I'm a web designer and I have used social media in various ways. Information, answers, relaxation and interaction with the famous, the "slightly famous" and the not famous at all.

I attended a two-day, online industry conference in 2010 and chatted on Twitter with many of the attendees. Following the conference, many of the folks I had exchanged tweets with thought it would be great to keep the conversation going. We arranged to chat online the following Wednesday at noon, and have been doing this weekly for three years. Over the years we've coached and encouraged each other, polished our LinkedIn profiles, worked on projects together, and held each other up during various family problems and the loss of a spouse.

I've often gotten business through relationships developed and nurtured online, or as a referral from someone I've met online. I've reconnected with folks from high school, and even elementary school, and built websites for them. This may have been partly because of our shared connections, but mainly through demonstrating knowledge, helpfulness and authenticity through actively engaging each other through social media.

These real connections were established or re-established through the "magic" of social media. But there's really no magic. The same skills you learned in kindergarten apply online. You should be kind to both friends and strangers. Sharing is still important. You should remember to say please, and when someone does something nice for you, remember to say thank you.

Social media isn't new or hard. The same business skills and good graces you use offline apply online. Maybe they're even more important online, because 140 characters live forever on the Internet.

#3: My Big Safety Statement

"Never do, say, or engage in social media in a way you don't want to be seen, heard or perceived in life."

~ @NCWiseman

This is my big safety statement.

The moment we do something, say something or engage in something foolish, our connections will think differently of us. Making these mistakes can blemish, if not critically destroy our reputation and relationships.

It is highly probable that somewhere along the way, we will do, say, or engage in a manner we later determine is foolish. When we do, apply Dale Carnegie's principle #12, "If we are wrong, admit it quickly and emphatically." We must correct ourselves in public and apologize where and to whom it's appropriate. Then, never make that mistake again. Consider the mistake a learning event.

One way to reduce the chance of this mistake is to use Mayo Clinic's Social Media Policy:

- Don't Lie, Don't Pry
- Don't Cheat, Can't Delete
- Don't Steal, Don't Reveal

(Source - Google Mayo Clinic Social Media Policy)

If one of our social media posts contradicts this 12-word social media policy, we must delete it without hitting submit. If we've already hit submit, follow Dale Carnegie's principle #12.

#4: Everything you do must be TRUHE

"Everything we do on social media must be **TRUHE**. *If not, people will begin to ignore us."*

~ @NCWiseman

Because it is so important, let me repeat what TRUHE means:

- Transparent
- Relevant
- Useful
- Honest
- Engaging (Exciting or Entertaining)

During one of my community college classes, Thelma Elaine Carter helped me build the acronym TRUHE. While teaching the importance of being Transparent, Relevant, Useful and Honest, I jokingly called it TRUH. I spelled it out loud for the class.

Elaine raised her hand and politely corrected me, "Teddy, you spelled true incorrectly." We laughed together knowing Elaine was correct.

Later in the class I said I wanted to add an "E" to TRUH because Engaging is just as important as Transparent, Relevant, Useful and Honest. Again Elaine raised her hand to correct me. This time she said, "You're getting closer to spelling true correctly Teddy." Again we all laughed together.

Thank you Elaine for helping me to build **TRUHE**. It is now one of my Life Principles that is very relevant to our use of social media.

Imagine when we all speak and share TRUHE content, every day in every post and statement. The world will be a far better place, and as individuals we'll also be far better off. TRUHE has so much value when using social media as well as in real life. Go back to the chapter on TRUHE if you want to refresh yourself on this.

Pause and take a moment to read a Social Media Success Story

Marcy Lucas Success Story

linkedin.com/in/marcylucas

LinkedIn played a big part in my last two career changes.

Story # 1 - Using my networking skills, I reached out to those I have worked with in the past, and others who I have connected with during my multiple job search adventures. Many of these people I looked for and found on LinkedIn first. A recruiter found my profile on LinkedIn and contacted me regarding a position in Denver, Colorado. Although the job was a good fit, I did not want to move to Colorado. I forwarded the job description to previous co-workers in Texas, Oklahoma, and Pennsylvania, to see if they knew anyone who would be interested. One of my connections replied to me with an idea regarding opportunities open in her department, working remotely. I was trying to help others and she turned the help around to help me. When I sent her my resume she forwarded it to the hiring manager, (her manager) who set up an interview with me and three others. I checked my LinkedIn contacts, so see who possibly knew the people who were going to be interviewing me. In addition to my friend's referral, I quickly was able to find two other people who were willing to contact the interviewers with recommendations. I got the job and started soon thereafter.

Story # 2 - Even though I do not have my PMP certification, Teddy Burriss suggested that I attend the local chapter meetings of the Project Management Institute. During the meeting I realized that this was a great group of people with similar interests and backgrounds. I enjoyed the food, networking, and the various speakers. I even reconnected with some previous co-workers and we connected via LinkedIn as well. One of these friends introduced me to a recruiter. After, I shared my history and goals, she thought of a position that would be a good match, not even knowing if there was an opening. Soon afterwards, an interview was set up and I was hired as a contractor as a Project Delivery Coordinator in a large IT department.

LinkedIn played a big part in each of these stories. I am convinced that the stories would have either turned out differently or taken much longer to develop if it were not for LinkedIn.

I enjoy networking and continue to add to my LinkedIn contacts. It provides additional incentive to potentially help connect others who are looking for new opportunities.

#5: Live by the 5Cs of Social Media

"To get the greatest value out of social media, we must execute the 5 Cs of Contribute, Collaborate, Connect, Cram and Create."

~ @NCWiseman

Like TRUHE, I believe the 5Cs are an important part of social media relationship-building. The 5Cs of social media are:

- Contribute
- Collaborate
- Connect
- Cram
- Create

I think these 5Cs are encompassing of all the activities we must do on social media in order to build meaningful relationships and be considered someone who can be trusted and is respected as an authority in our niche.

Because I feel that social media is an extension of our IRL activities, the 5Cs apply to real life as well.

Go back to the chapter on the 5Cs of Social Media if you want to refresh yourself on this principle.

#6: Become trusted, respected and cared for

"We must always have trust, respect, and compassion for our connections. Otherwise they won't want to have trust, respect and compassion for us."

~ @NCWiseman

Far too often, I see people fail because of the way they treat their contacts. Some people don't understand the value of caring for their connections in life or on social media.

I've seen people carry around their stack of business cards and eagerly share the phone numbers and email addresses with "vultures" who want to cold call these unsuspecting folks. No polite introduction or consideration of relevance, just sharing contact info. For this reason, many people don't like to network or connect on social media. They are afraid of the business card vultures.

I've had people email, message or call me and say, "Hey Teddy, you're connected to such and such, would you connect me to them? I need an "in" to their business so I can sell my stuff." (Not the exact words, but close.)

I've seen people add their connections to mailing lists, invite them to irrelevant events, let others ask for irrelevant or selfish introductions, and tag them on posts that are not appropriate. Each of these is a selfish misuse of their connections.

I want my connections to trust, respect, and care for

me, so I try never to treat them disrespectfully. We should all want our connections to treat us in a respectful way. It starts with us. Only share connections with others when there is a TRUHE and mutually beneficial reason to do so.

Respecting our connections shows we care about them and appreciate them, regardless of how great or simple the relationship is. This is how we become trusted, respected and cared for in life, career, business and community.

Pause and take a moment to read a Social Media Success Story

John Lusher Success Story

@JohnLusher

johnlusher.com

linkedin.com/in/johnlusher

June 29, 2011 was a hard day personally for me. I attended the funeral of a friend and former co-worker that left us much too soon. Dealing with the mix of emotions and sadness, I did what we all have to do at times, put a brave face on and carry on. That same evening, I was joining colleagues and friends for a social media meetup in Floyd, VA. This was the inaugural event for the group in Floyd, and as one of the founding members of our local Roanoke VA meetup group, I was excited to attend their event, albeit with sadness in my heart.

Despite my hurting, I joined my friends along with other good people for the event. The networking and time with friends felt good. It felt right.

Fast forward a couple of hours until time for us to leave. When my friend started paying their bills for the night, our waitress asked, who is John Lusher? I admitted it was me, and she stated that my check had been already been paid by someone. I asked my friends and they knew nothing about it. Our waitress said a lady called in and paid for my meal and drinks. She couldn't remember the name but said something about the person being from the north. We were thinking a friend of mine in Canada had done it until the waitress mentioned something about it being the Jewelry lady! I knew instantly it was my friend, Julianne Paulsen, (@YRJewelryGal) owner of Viaggiao Bracelets.

On the drive back, I called Julianne. Laughter is all I heard as she answered the phone. Laughter from both of us. She knew exactly why I was calling. Julianne had seen my posts on Facebook that day about my friends funeral service along with our networking event that evening. She decided to do a little something to lift my spirits by buying my dinner and drinks. The funny thing is, she had to Google the name of the restaurant we were at, call them and convince them she wasn't a nut and wanted to pay for my meal! The footnote to this story happened in 2012 when I was in California for the Orange County Social Media Summit; we repeated the process. With my full knowledge Julianne paid for one of my meals, to show another friend the power of social connections and how they can enrich our lives.

Paying for my meal is not the story. This story is about how a social networking connection, turns into a life-long friendship. Julianne had been a friend for a while before this all happened. We originally connected on Twitter then on Facebook. Today she is a dear and close friend. This is why social media is so vital; it provides a way to connect to people that you otherwise may not meet and when you nurture the relationship it can develop into a life long friendship.

#7: It's not all about you

"If everything we do is all about us, then success is less likely to occur. Make life mutually beneficial and life will be far more rewarding."

~ @NCWiseman

This principle applies to our activities on social media as well as IRL. Fortunately we can tell who is only using social media to promote themselves, their business or missions. Their profiles and pages are nothing but sales material and promotional content.

Selfishness is a character flaw in life as well as in social media activity. In real life we try to minimize our involvement with these people. On social media we end up hiding or disconnecting from these profiles or pages.

When we have permission, it's OK to talk about ourselves a little in a discussion, but when the entire conversation is only all about us, that's just not going to work. It causes the quality of relationships to diminish and social media engagement comes to a grinding stop. Dale Carnegie taught us through his Principle # 8, "Talk in terms of the other person's interest." This works IRL and on social media too.

When we make our conversations, posts, comments, etc more about the other person, our social media engagement and relationships will grow.

#8: Giving is a Relationship Tool

"Giving is a powerful way to build relationship, whether in real life or through social media."

~ @NCWiseman

I make money by giving and sharing.

This is not a selfish thing or an ego thing; it's just real. I've found over and over again that when I give with no strings attached and no expectations, I am rewarded. The rewards are broad and diverse, and sometimes they have nothing to do with revenue. Yet the rewards are measurable and with a good degree of regularity, they show up in the form of revenue. This is good, because after all, I do run a business.

Giving through social media is easy to do. I've made a significant number of fruitful relationships because I focus on giving first. The people who connect with me and then begin to engage with me do so because I share (give) all the time.

My giving is not my products and services, but rather, useful—TRUHE—information and activities that my connections benefit from. (See the chapters on Contribute and Collaborate for a refresher on giving.)

It may be hard to believe that giving with no expectations is a powerful way to build relationships, until after you start doing this.

Yes, I know, lots of people will want this conversation to come back to money. I make money because of my giving through social media. However, for me, the rewards are far greater than just the money.

Money is the least beneficial reason to give. Call it a God thing, Karma, or just life, giving works, and it works just as well through social media as it does IRL.

This giving philosophy has changed my life and can change yours as well.

Pause and take a moment to read a Social Media Success Story

by Teddy Burriss

Eric Melniczek Success Story

@EricMelniczek

linkedin.com/in/ericmelniczek

Hello

In March 2009, my wife, Amanda, sent me an e-mail message for a position to serve as the Director of Career & Internship Services at High Point University in High Point, North Carolina. My wife and I were living in Radford, Virginia which is approximately two hours from High Point, North Carolina.

Although, I was 35 years old at the time, I had never been to High Point in my life. While my network included a lot of career planning and development professionals, I did not know anyone personally at High Point University.

My first act of business was to identify, using LinkedIn, the individual who had previously served in the Director role. I found her LinkedIn profile and sent her a message introducing myself & asking her if she would be open to having a conversation with me about her time at High Point University as well as sharing some market intelligence with regard to the culture of High Point University. She was working and living in the Triad and we had a great telephone conversation followed by several e-mail exchanges. She was most helpful.

From there, I spoke with some professionals in the North Carolina Association of Colleges and Employers (NCACE) to find out more about the Piedmont Triad and High Point University. All of them were very helpful.

In the end, I utilized LinkedIn to get introduced to career planning and development professionals who were instrumental in my decision to accept the offer with HPU!

#9: A Connection does not make a Relationship

"A connection does not make a relationship. Relationships occur when we help others."

~ @NCWiseman

Furthermore, relationships are needed for mutually beneficial value to occur both IRL as well as through social media.

Another way to say this important quote as it relates to business is:

"A connection does not make a relationship. A relationship is needed for rewarding business to occur. Make connections, develop relationship, create business opportunities."

~ @NCWiseman

Far too often I see people connecting on social media with no desire to truly focus on building relationships. This does not work.

I regularly get a LinkedIn connection request that includes a request to talk business before the requestor truly knows who I am. To me, this is like cold calling or sending SPAM emails, neither of which are acceptable to me.

In my first book, "*Networking for Mutual Benefit,*" I shared the story of how one of my bosses told me I would be successful at sales if I, "gripped and grinned my way through networking events, collected as many business cards as possible, then called those people to tell them about our products." I knew (and proved) this is not very successful in real life, and it will not be very successful on social media either.

The people who focus first on getting to know me have a greater opportunity of getting value from our connection, maybe even eventually doing business with me.

Again, trust me on this one: a connection does not make a relationship, and you need to build relationships before you can ask for anything.

When you make connections and develop relationships, opportunities will present themselves. Often these opportunities come from connections you never imagined they would come from. It works.

#10: Always be yourself

"Never contradict who we are or what we stand for when using social media."

~ @NCWiseman

If we present ourselves one way on one social media platform and differently on another, we could be considered fake.

Likewise, if IRL we act differently than we do on social media, we could be labeled fake.

The moment someone learns we are not real, they will ignore us. This will stifle, if not end, our ability to create relationships that could become beneficial at some time.

I strive to be Teddy at all times. I believe most people trust and respect me for who I am, what I do, how I act and what I stand for. It also makes it easier to engage on social media in a consistent manner. I never have to consider, "Who am I today?" or "On what social media platform should I talk this way?"

A few years ago, a friend wanted to create a hidden Facebook group to tell jokes he wouldn't tell in public. He asked me to teach him how to setup this group. I advised him not to do this. I showed him how he could easily make a mistake and post a bad joke in the wrong place and ruin every relationship he had been working to develop. He wisely opted not to create this hidden group.

As long as we follow the principles of TRUHE, we can have a consistent public personality. It's far easier, safer, and authentic.

My good friend Dr Seuss told me years ago (yeah, through his books), "Today you are You, that is truer than true. There is no one alive who is Youer than You." Please, always be the best you can be, IRL and on social media.

Pause and take a moment to read a Social Media Success Story

Cyndi Briggs Success Story

@DrCyndiBriggs

drcyndibriggs.com

linkedin.com/in/cyndibriggs

The heavy box was postmarked Switzerland.

Who do I know in Switzerland? I wondered. I've never even been to Switzerland.

Inside, a treasure trove of Swiss chocolates and a handmade paper bead necklace. And a card. Thanking me. For my writing, my message to the world, and my intention to be of service. From a woman I've never met outside of social media and blogging, who connects with me in a real and soulful way.

Chocolates from Maya. A book from Elizabeth in Virginia. Thank you notes from Mo in Australia and Catherine in New York and many others. A network of hearts beating around the globe, all of us seeking connection and purpose. Showing up for each other in the virtual world.

When I began blogging back in 2009, I did so with trepidation. I'm a private person, an introvert at heart, and I hesitated to share my story with a world that might not receive it with grace or kindness. Plus, I harbored a vague, nagging fear about weirdoes. Internet stalking is a thing, right?

But, like most writers, I felt I had a message to share. Words bubbled up inside of me, insisting on expression. I needed to write about the things in life that really matter, like purpose and meaning and the fleeting, tenuous nature of it all. As I struggled with my existential questions, I observed others around me searching just as intently for their own answers. I felt deeply that through writing my story, I might be of service to others.

I took to WordPress and Facebook and Twitter, anonymously at first and then publicly, gaining courage as connections built. I started receiving emails from readers, sharing their own stories and thanking me for mine. It was astounding to me, how quickly and completely my words connected us, like dots on paper waiting for a child's crayon to transform us into a vibrant work of art.

Similarly, I reached out to my own writing and creative heroes: Patti Digh, Susan Piver, Andrea Schroeder. I am still quietly awed when they respond to my Tweets and Facebook comments, all of us equal on this digital playing field. How amazing to so instantly and easily connected with like-minded souls. And how comforting to feel less alone as a writer, an inherently lonely process.

In the end, it's not about the chocolates. Nor the thank you notes. Nor the business I attract without even a hint of creepy, sales-y marketing. I blog and use social media because it breaks down barriers between people, erases geographic boundaries, and allows a writer with a day job (like me) a platform for dreaming and creative expression. This is my success: that I have bound myself, heart to heart, with my tribe.

#11: Bonus - Experience and Experiment

> *"Experience and Experiment without giving up; this is the best way to discover how social media can benefit us and our companies."*
>
> ~ @NCWiseman

I created this principle after being asked, "How do I figure out how to use social media?"

Yes, you can read lots of books and even attend seminars and training sessions. I encourage you to read good books and attend good seminars. However like lots of other things in life, we learn best by actually doing.

Experimenting with techniques, ideas, tips, and tricks is one of the best ways to learn new things. Riding bikes, skiing, snowboarding, using a Smartphone, and even skydiving are all learned best by doing (more than once). This is true with social media as well.

Get a little coaching, as you are doing by reading this book, then Experience and Experiment!

The opportunities to create success will multiply just because we dared to try.

Paying Attention on Social Media

pay·ing at·ten·tion /paying/ /ə 'tenSHən/ - adjective

1. Taking heed

2. giving close and thoughtful attention;

"An expert is someone who has succeeded in making decisions and judgements simpler through knowing what to pay attention to and what to ignore." - Edward de Bono

"Tell me to what you pay attention and I will tell you who you are." - Jose Ortega y Gasset

"We really teach ourselves. If you want to learn, you will always find someone to learn from, be they dead or alive, great or unknown. You learn from everything you see and hear around you - if you are willing to pay attention." - Alexander Volkov

"Social media contains a wealth of information. We need to pay attention to the important stuff."

~ @NCWiseman

Social media platforms contain lots of words of wisdom from smart people who like to share what they have learned from others. Articles, info-graphics, videos, charts, tables, quotes, links to books and seminars, workshops and conferences. Then we have communities and groups that focus their discussions, philosophies, ideas and discoveries on a single topic, issue, product, business or group of people. The list of social media information is extensive and continues to grow.

There are three things we need to know about this wealth of knowledge.

- Some of the content found on social media may be useful to us.

- Some of the content found on social media may not be useful to us.

- Some of the content found on social media is untrue.

Whether on Facebook, Twitter, LinkedIn, Google+, Pinterest, Instagram, blogs or any other platform, we need to pay attention to what is useful to us, ignore what is not and always consider, maybe even challenge, the source and validity of the content.

The social media content we should pay attention to includes:

- New useful and interesting content about our industry

- New ideas that can help us in our career, business or community

- Interesting, engaging and even entertaining content we enjoy and/or can benefit from

The social media content we should ignore includes:

- Old content about our industry

- Old ideas that can't help us in our career, business or community

- Content that is self serving, one sided and/or not entertaining to us

Beyond TRUHE content, there are activities on social media we should also pay attention to. Here are a few activities to pay attention to:

- Who has viewed our LinkedIn Profiles
- Who regularly shares and engages on our content
- Who subscribes to our blogs, Facebook and YouTube Channels and LinkedIn Company Pages
- What our competitors and/or peers are doing on social media and what kinds of engagement their activities create

The types of activities and content on social media will continue to change as the social media platforms change. Again, what we need to do is to pay attention to the useful and interesting content and where relevant and useful, consume it for our benefit and share it for the benefit of our connections. Paying attention to social media content can help us to build relationships with the content authors and the people we share it with.

Paying attention is not just something we should have done in high school and college, it's something we have to continue doing in life as we find new ways to connect and build relationships in real life and through social media.

Pause and take a moment to read a Social Media Success Story

David Scheumann Success Story

@scheumannCPA

scheumanncpa.com

linkedin.com/in/scheumanncpa

From September 2009 to September 2011 my CPA Firm business nearly doubled.

Twitter and Facebook alone brought in 35-40% of this new business. I met lots of great people through Twitter. Some absolutely great clients who are now good friends. These connections then referred me to lots of new business, tax clients and PT-CFO clients.

The funny thing is I resisted social media like the plague for a couple of years. Thought it was just stupid. And of course, generally speaking, my profession does not like change and the thoughts within my profession are that social media is stupid.

One day I was talking to a friend who is a car salesman. He was telling me about how his sales are up...but workload was down. He was making connections via social media and as friends of friends (and/or tweeps) would be looking to buy a car, people would recommend him. So, 1) people were coming to the car dealer and specifically asking for him, or scheduling appointments with him, 2) he was finding out exactly what people wanted before they got there and had numerous cars lined up and ready and 3) he sold a few cars virtually, except for signing the final papers and delivery. Often he never met the customer IRL.

So, I decided to give it a whirl. BUT, I was only going to use it for business! I would tweet out tax tips, topics, reminders, etc. That was it.

Well, I had some followers and had some folks reply from time to time about the tweets. But no real business growth. Then my more social side kicked in and I started to actually interact with people. Folks started asking about services. A few folks asked me to do guest blog posts and speak at lunches/dinners. As you can imagine, that is when I started to see business growth. So I really started to embrace it and continued to see even more growth in my business.

Now, back to my profession not liking social media. I was at a continuing education event a year or so ago. I was sitting with a group at lunch and the topic of business development came up. A few of the guys were complaining that they have done ads in phonebooks, ads in local magazines, direct mail, discounts to new customers, etc, etc with little to no business growth. So, I spoke up and openly admitting to not only having Twitter/Facebook accounts, but that I actually use them.

Before I could explain what it had done for my business, I was told just how stupid it was. Now I know what it would be like to don a UNC sweatshirt and walk through the Duke campus.

The guy sitting next to me (one of the main complainers) just started ripping on me and Facebook. "I would NEVER accept a client looking for a CPA on Facebook! NEVER! I don't have time for that crap. I don't care if someone is getting dinner at xyz restaurant. Blah. Blah. Blah."

Once they were all done chastising me, I reminded them how they were all complaining about not seeing results from all of their marketing efforts. I asked them how much had they spent on the Yellow Pages ad, the direct mail pieces – both in production and mailing the post cards. I then explained how I had seen real results that I can link directly to social media. I explained to the guy "that would never accept a client looking for a CPA on Facebook" that I bill several of these clients that he would "never accept" more than he spent on his entire direct mail campaign.

Before I excused myself from the table, I had one more comment....Oh, by the way – IT IS FREE!!

I am so glad that I have decided to get engaged on social media. Building relationships that open doors to business for my CPA Firm.

Dealing with Fear and Risk

risk [risk] *noun*

1. exposure to the chance of injury or loss; a hazard o
r dangerous chance

fear [feer] noun

1. distressing emotion aroused by impending danger,
evil, pain, etc.

"Go for it, while you can. I know you have it in you. And I can't promise you'll get everything you want, but I can promise nothing will change if you don't try." ~ J.M. Darhower, Sempre

"When you take risks you learn that there will be times when you succeed and there will be times when you fail, and both are equally important." ~ Ellen DeGeneres, Seriously...I'm Kidding

"Be wise enough not to be reckless, but brave enough to take great risks." ~ Frank Warren

> *"Never do, say, or engage in social media in a way you don't want to be seen, heard or perceived in life."*
>
> ~ @NCWiseman

There are lots of people afraid to use social media. Here are the top five reasons:

Fear #1 - "What happens if I say the wrong thing or worse yet, I say or do something stupid?"

Fear #2 - "It's a compliance issue. Social media activity is contradictory to FINRA."

Fear #3 - "What happens if an employee says something that could damage the reputation of my company?"

Fear #4 - "I don't want the world to know everything about me. I don't want my personal business out there for everyone to see."

Fear #5 - "My employees will just play games. I don't see any business value at all."

To some degree or another, all of these fears are real. It's one of my missions in life to educate people how to manage the fears and mitigate the risks of using social media for life, career, business, and community. It can be done, and it is worth the time and effort.

When Samuel Morse created the telegraph, I wonder if someone was afraid a message would be sent that shouldn't have been.

What about the first telephone conversations, or the first television or radio broadcasts? How about the first billboards, or Super Bowl ads? Did the folks involved in these different medias fear a mistake or the wrong message being sent out? I'm sure they did.

There's no question that few things of significant value to our lives come without some risk and a little fear. We must learn to harness the fear and manage the risks.

Beyond reading Dale Carnegie's book, *"How to stop worrying and start living,"* there are other things we can do to get past these fears and mitigate the risks:

1.Remember social media platforms are nothing

more than places to have conversations. Where else do we have conversations? In a client's office, at a coffee shop, on the 17th hole, standing on a street corner or sitting on bar stool number 5. Apply the TRUHE principle, and any conversation we are willing to have in a public place can be had on social media.

2. If we won't waste our time on the telephone, fax, email, or Skype, we should not waste time on social media. Focus on being productive and having meaningful conversations, regardless of what social media you're using. Use the principles we discussed under the chapter about Creating to manage your time.

3. We all make mistakes. It's a fact of life. So, if we say something we wish we had not said on social media, we have to deal with it. Delete it, correct it, and admit emphatically you were wrong to everyone your mistake affected. Then, never make that mistake again. This is one way we learn to be better.

4. Remember the TRUHE principle. Everything we do, say, and engage in on social media must be Transparent, Relevant, Useful, Honest, Engaging/Exciting/Entertaining. Before we hit that submit button always ask this question, "Is this TRUHE?" This helps to reduce potential big mistakes.

5. Remember this principle, "Never do, say or engage in social media in a way you don't want to be seen, heard or perceived in life." ~ @NCWiseman. When we stand this principle up next to TRUHE, the safety net this creates will nearly wipe out all the potential risks and

associated fears most people have with social media

6. If you don't want the world to know everything about you, don't share all of it on social media. Only share what you're comfortable sharing and with the people you are comfortable sharing with.

7. Learn! One way we get good at using a new tool is to learn how to use it. Attend a local seminar; participate in a webinar or two; read some good articles or book. Learn the details of the different areas of the social media tools you want to use. Stay informed of the changes and ask questions. If you have employees, teach them to use these tools properly. Share with them what you expect, require and what your goals are. If we don't teach our employees how to do it correctly, we'll always hide behind compliance departments and irrelevant doctrines.

8. Experiment and experience. Often doing this, even in the safest of ways, helps reduce the fear we have.

9. Believe in yourself! Often we don't do something new or different because we fear mistakes that actually never occur. When I studied the Dale Carnegie principles, I realized this quote is true, "99% of what we are afraid of never happens."

10. If you have employees, trust that they actually have the organization's best interest in mind when they are engaged in conversations on social media, or on the 19th hole or on bar stool # 17. If they're good employees and you've trained them properly, their use of social media shouldn't be a significant risk.

"We can reduce our fear and mitigate the risk of using social media if we follow the principles and ideas this book shares."

~ @NCWiseman

Let's Bring It All Home

The many social media platforms available to us, the connections we can make through them, and the content available to us through them, can provide value in our lives, careers, businesses, and communities.

To get the best value from our time using these communication tools, we need to follow the many principles, recommendations and ideas I have outlined in this book.

Here are the highlights:

- Networking for Mutual Benefit is a requirement for Success using Social Media.

- Never do, say or engage in social media in a way we don't want to be seen, heard or perceived in life.

- Everything we do on social media must be TRUHE: Transparent, Relevant, Useful, Honest and Engaging. If not, people will begin to ignore us.

- To get the greatest value out of social media, we must execute the 5Cs: Contribute, Collaborate, Connect, Cram and Create

- We must always have trust, respect, and compassion for our connections. Otherwise, they won't want to trust, respect, or have compassion for us.

- If everything we share on social media and life is all about us, then success is less likely to occur. Make social media content and life mutually beneficial, and life will be far richer.

- Giving is a powerful way to build relationship, whether in real life or through social media.

- A connection does not make a relationship. Relationships occur when we help others.

- Never contradict who we are or what we stand for when using social media.

- Experience and experiment without giving up. This is the best way to discover how social media can benefit us in life, career, business or community.

- Networking is finding, developing and nurturing relationships that mutually move people forward through life.

- Social media contains a wealth of information. We should pay attention to the important stuff.

- We can reduce our fear and mitigate the risk of using social media if we follow the principles and ideas from this book.

Congratulations! You have read this entire book.

I hope I've answered this question, "If I want to create success in my life, career, business and community, how should I be using social media?"

Social media is one of the newest communication tools available to us. It is unlikely to completely replace older communication tools (yet), but it's important to learn how to use the old and the new together for maximum impact. Where beneficial and appropriate, we need to adopt our lives to these new tools. Despite the fact that social media tools will change fast and furiously, they are not going away, and their value will continue to grow as they evolve.

Thanks for letting me share this book with you. I am blessed being able to share my ideas and experiences.

Additionally I am grateful that I may have a positive impact on your use of social media tools to create your success.

If we have not met yet, I look forward to meeting you somewhere in the near future, maybe IRL, maybe on social media. When we do, let's strike up a great conversation.

I share Social Media best practices, principles, guidance and training on the website www.ncwiseman.com

Visit me there. Consider joining the mailing list and continue to learn more ways to create *"Success using Social Media."*

And most of all, have fun doing it.

Teddy

Pause and take a moment to read my Social Media Success Story

Teddy Burriss Success Story

@TLBurriss

NCWiseman.com

linkedin.com/in/tlburriss

I have hundreds of social media success stories. Twitter connections that have turned into good personal friends, LinkedIn connections who read what I share and refer or hired me for consulting and public speaking, Facebook connections that have helped me personally or helped my unemployed friends, Foursquare connections who offered me business opportunities or volunteered for my charitable projects, as well as blog followers who have become business partners.

I purposely did not include my Social Media Success Stories in this book because I wanted you to read the stories from other social media users.

However, I have to share this Social Media Success Story.

I reached out through Twitter, LinkedIn, Facebook and Google+ asking for the success stories that I are scattered out in this book. I got dozens of responses and through the discussions about these stories, I met dozens of new people.

The people I talked with, many I don't see often, some I've never met IRL, were all eager to help me with this book. Some of the people I talked with told me that I needed to meet others with great stories. I met with these folks, listened to their stories, and created some great relationships with these new connections.

I got the opportunity to meet people I would never had reached out to, if not for the recommendations of my social media connections.

Thanks to my social media friend, Elizabeth Cottrell, who I have not yet met IRL, for asking me if she could be my editor, not for the money, but because she believes in my message and lives it every day of her life.

I am grateful for every person I talked with and especially the fabulous folks who shared their story for this book and for my collection of Social Media Success Stories that I now publish on NCWiseman.com.

Made in the USA
Charleston, SC
15 July 2014